Praise for *Before the Age of Reason: A Memoir of Racism*

"She captures a child's confusion at the casual even jocular racism of the home and her awakening to it in the world. What these stories have to say in their vivid succinct way is that racism is systemic."
 -Hanford Woods

"Anyone born before the Civil Rights era will instantly relate to Mimi Morton's riveting memoir about racism, sexism, religious and class prejudice. With startling detail and wit, Morton evokes her societal coming-of-age and prods us to rethink our own."
 -Pamela Thomas, author of *Fatherless Daughters: Turning the Pain of Loss into the Power of Forgiveness*

"Mimi Morton grows up in the U.S. mess of inherited racism mixed with guilt, love, gossip, sex, described in precise language, including many generations-old, now mostly lost, sayings.
This wonder-filled memoir opens a door. Go in. Read it."
 -Kathryn Kilgore, writer and poet

"Morton's eloquently written and perspicuous memoir of the subtle (and not so subtle) influences of racism, candidly explores the author's developing consciousness from childhood innocence and adolescent shame, to eventual awareness and responsibility. *Before the Age of Reason* is a must-read in our time of national awakening."
 -Robin Westen, award-winning journalist

BEFORE THE AGE OF REASON

BEFORE THE AGE OF REASON

A Memoir of Racism

MIMI MORTON

Burlington, Vermont

Copyright © 2020 by Mimi Morton

All rights reserved. No part of this publication may be reproduced, distri-buted, or transmitted in any form or by any means, including photocopying, recording, or other electronic or mechanical methods, without the prior written permission of the publisher, except in the case of brief quotations embodied in critical reviews and certain other noncommercial uses permitted by copyright law.

ISBN: 978-1-949066-64-7
Library of Congress Control Number: 2020922223

Onion River Press
191 Bank Street
Burlington, VT 05401

For my darling Rick and our grandsons,
Jesse and Orion

Contents

Prologue		xi
Introduction		1
1	Bread and Gravy	3
2	Black and White Photo	6
3	Diversity in the Family	10
4	A Child's Garden of Diversity	14
5	Race Riot	19
6	Dentistry	24
7	Penn Street	28
8	Shine	31
9	Home Schooling	33
10	Belle	38
11	Names	40
12	Conservative	44

13	Snow Day	49
14	Peach Street	53
15	PHS	58
16	Going South	65
17	The Other Black	67
18	The Underground	70
19	The Other Rosenberg	72
20	The Prince	76
21	Afro	81
22	Electric Carving Knife	83
23	Blackstone Rangers	87
24	Cigar Ash	91
25	Midwest	95
26	Montreal	98
27	Vermont	108
28	Twin	112
29	Cyberspace	114

Acknowledgements — 117
About The Author — 119

Prologue

My work was inspired by *"The 1619 Project"* of the *New York Times* (published August, 2019). *"1619"* brought together reflections on race and racism by artists and writers, and brilliant revisionist history by contemporary African American intellectuals. It woke me to my ignorance about our history. I was taught that racism ended with the Civil War. *"The 1619 Project"* showed that the system of racism has not died but continues now. These revelations motivated me to bear witness to my own racism by dredging for my memories from earliest childhood to the present.

In the context of our current national situation, some of the scenes I chronicle may appear almost benign. A pre-digital time of social repression. Now, as police murder of African Americans continues, the country rages, drifts, flails without a functioning government. The Buddhist triad of ignorance, hatred, and greed have been unleashed and condoned by our elected officials and their supporters.

If we are going to save democracy, we must acknowledge the legacy of racism that brought us to this moment and that underlies the attitudes of most white people, including well-meaning liberals who claim not to be racists.

White people have a responsibility to hold themselves to account for their own racism. This memoir is my attempt to do so. I have tried to see clearly the racism that formed me, and its continuation into the present. Only by being conscious can I change and contribute to a more just society.

Introduction

Mimi Morton grew up in South Jersey, the Garden State. The family processed summer fruit after dinner as Mimi listened to stories spiked with criticism about social and cultural difference. Moving through her small town, and then beyond it, she saw herself an outsider, intelligent, capable, but often outside the action.

Mimi began writing this memoir in 2019, as African-American writers and protestors in the streets unraveled the narrative of "our" United States, revealing its historic racist agenda. She realized that the "beautiful projects" many of us had embraced, the women's movement, the anti-war movement, the years on the commune, and the organic food movement, failed to challenge systemic racism. Good intentions and harm reduction programs were not enough now. Writing "Before the Age of Reason" has required humility and stamina. Luckily, she has welcomed us to join her.

-Verandah Porche, Total Loss Farm, Guilford, Vermont

I

Bread and Gravy

The end of a roast beef dinner. Almost a weekly occurrence in our house, that or chicken. The dining room, across the front hall from the living room, nailed down the first floor. The center of action. Two windows. Venetian blinds. Corner cupboards. A chandelier, modest, not dangling, but providing the overhead glare suitable for domestic interrogation. A painted Sarouk Persian rug on the floor, probably bought by my grandfather when he moved his family into the house in 1920. As the family entered the 1960's, candles to keep pace with the softer glow emanating from the hated Kennedy administration.

I sat beside my grandfather, source of all good things, my link to the old ways. "Make a light," he'd say when he walked into a dark room. "That's a nice waist," he'd compliment me on a blouse. "Get a nigger off the street," he'd say echoing early 20th century Philadelphia, when he was short of laborers on a building job.

I heard this at the dinner table. *Get a nigger off the street.* Sign of a simpler time before unions, before heroin but not before black men were seen outside and out of work. *Get a nigger off the street*, spoken with an edge of humor, nostalgia. This is how things were.

I didn't know what Jim Crow meant. Had never heard the term. I'd never heard of lynching but I'd heard of Lynchburg, Virginia, where a classmate's mother was born. Later, the Rosenbergs, the electric chair, Joe McCarthy was mentioned in the kitchen. My parents were drinking rye and soda or gin and tonic, depending on the season, while my mother made dinner. Sometimes they listened to a comical record called *Point of Order* that my father brought home and played on the record player. I didn't understand it.

Later, when my father took over my grandfather's business, he ran a union shop, bought his own tools back out of hock when they were stolen off a job site, bailed out a laborer if he was drunk and disorderly. A benevolent employer. Paternalistic. "Mister Jim," his laborer Shelly called him. "'Shel,'" my father quoted himself in one of his dinner table stories. "'Where you been, Shel?'" Shelly tells the story of what happened at his girlfriend's, the conclusion of which stayed with me: "'I could not deny that child.'" Born out of wedlock, my mother said. The poor but happy lives of the colored people.

"Oh nothing," my mother described a summer Saturday evening in a phone call to her sister. "We're just lolling around here in our happy African fashion." This was Mother evoking her version of African tribal life: grass skirts, grass huts, laziness.

Lolling around was not permitted in our family unless accompanied by a high ball.

I liked the crusty outer layer of roast beef with a bit of the pure fat crackling. If I was newly recovered from a flu, downstairs at family dinner for the first time in a few days, my grandfather might cut up my meat and feed me. I was six. Before the age of reason according to the Catholic church. I hadn't yet committed a sin. I'd been baptized so I wouldn't go to Limbo, if I died each night, which I feared, from listening to the pounding in my ear against the pillow, not knowing that it was my heart but imagining that my brain was trying to escape.

"Honeybunch," my grandfather said, offering a forkful of meat.

Get a nigger off the street.

2

Black and White Photo

My fraternal twin brother Jimmy and I grew up in the house my grandfather had built, that my mother was raised in. Rivertown was a resort for 19th century Philadelphians, bounded by the Delaware River on the west, a golf course on the east, a "crick" on the north and a working class market town on the south.

My first memories were black and white with a sepia wash around incandescent light bulbs: the hospital in Camden where my brother and I had our tonsils removed when we were three. The black and white ride home in our father's '49 Ford. I sat on my mother's lap in the front seat and vomited on the dashboard. The bare winter trees and the steam locomotive that passed in a stream of black and white at the bottom of our street. We stayed home with our mother and we rarely went anywhere in our father's car except to see our Aunt Matty in the next town and Aunt Lou outside of Philadelphia. Only radio. The sound of football or baseball games in the background.

The streets were quiet. Cars sometimes parked in front of houses or emerged from one-car garages. If our doctor's long yellow Cadillac—MD on the license plate—was parked in front of someone's house, we cringed. Sickness.

An elderly widower, Mr. Ewing, drove a pearl grey sedan. One hot August day, he came to swim in our little concrete pool, dug by my father. He wore beige swimming shoes and beige swimming trunks, and he carried a dish of chicken salad that he had bought at the luncheonette downtown. He 'took a dip' and then sat on the concrete edge and talked about someone who had to have a mole removed. Mr. Ewing was pale, old, rich. I listened to his story of the scary mole.

Our mother had prematurely grey hair cut short, sharp features to match her sharp words, pale green eyes. Her glare could reduce me to peeing in my pants. Our mother did not drive. We walked with her to the grocery store. We walked to church. We walked to the tiny library on Main St. and later we walked to school. We walked to the Fourth of July Parade and the Memorial Day parade and the Halloween Parade. We didn't see a black person. They must have existed but we didn't notice them. They had no reality. Shadows on the street or in the street sweeping, shoveling, mowing, digging.

The only black person I remember from those early years was Ada, the cleaning lady who came to our house once a week. Ada was tall and lean and wore dresses with belts and collars and she wore a hair net over straight black hair that was neither short nor long. Later our mother told me that Ada was a Gullah woman from the Sea Islands of Georgia. She went home every summer to visit and sent us postcards. One said, "Injoyn the fine weather." My mother showed me the card as a humorous display of Ada's simple education. My mother wasn't disparaging so much as pointing out folk phenomenon. In this, she was ahead of her time.

Ada ate lunch in the kitchen with us, sitting on a stool at the counter by the sink while my mother and brother and I ate at the table. I don't know if she brought lunch but I can imagine our mother making her whatever kind of sandwich she served us.

I don't remember seeing any other black person as a child until 4th grade when I became aware of Arthur Miner, a quiet boy who lived in a row house near school. Rivertown's version of a row house was a tall, single house connected to another house by a common wall. Just the two houses conjoined, what the English call 'semi-detached.'

As a child, I was alert to the signs of class difference. A house that had to share anything with another house—front yard, driveway, curb, tree—was showing economic weakness. Sharing meant there wasn't enough for each of you. As a twin, I was made aware of the risks of sharing every day.

A few row houses had been built on Main Street probably in the late 19th century. Today these houses are considered choice examples of heritage architecture, but at the time they were rented, like the brick apartments near the memorial park.

Divorced white women and families with low earning fathers lived in the apartments. As an adolescent, I visited a classmate in the apartments. Hers was the only working mother in the entire school, a badge of separateness. An old lady and her handsome bachelor son Randy—later I realized Randy was probably gay—lived next door. They invited us over to listen to the son play piano. I loved to visit them. Randy was witty and he treated us children as his equals. The world seemed to be more fun when he was around. I liked my friend June's mother for the same reason. She called us her "little people" which I took as a compliment.

3

Diversity in the Family

Catholics on my mother's side, Baptists and agnostics on my father's side comprised the religious diversity of my family until my paternal cousin and his wife took the trajectory from Agnosticism to Unitarianism to Amyway to AA to Born Again Christianity and the conservative politics that went with it. Eventually they dropped off the family roster beyond holiday emails.

Economic diversity was inevitable during the Depression and the 1950s when my father quietly supported his indigent mother and brother and a few divorced sisters before more solvent marriages got them back on their feet.

Racial diversity would have been unlikely had this not been America, where many families identified Native Americans somewhere in their rural 19th century background. By the 21st century some families identified African Americans in their geneology but my family was not one.

My father was of Scots descent. He spent his adolescence in Jockey Hollow, a nearly unpopulated location in the Southern Tier of New York State which I have never been able to locate on a map. He spoke of Clifford Cellam, a cousin who was, according to family lore, "crazy headed," my father's way of alluding to behaviors, particularly drunkenness, which indicated to my father and other relatives that Clifford carried Native American blood. Were alcoholism the mark of First Nation identity, nearly every man and woman in my father's family could be identified as Indians.

Unlike now, the early 20th century it was relatively easy to ascend in class. My mother's family was Methodist English until my grandmother married my Irish grandfather and converted to Catholicism. My grandfather worked his way up from bricklayer's apprentice to carpenter and finally to a partner in a building firm that he ultimately passed on to my father. Like my father, my grandfather supported his sisters when they were out of seamstress work or abandoned in marriage. The exception was his sister Mary, who married above herself, to a dentist. The dentist was South American, I was never told from which country, much as Americans have referred to Africa as a country rather than a continent. Dr. Andrade and his Irish-American wife lived in a four story brownstone on East 95th St in New York, where my mother spent several magical Christmases (servants, lighted candles on a towering fir tree, midnight mass at St Patrick's Cathedral transported in a hansom cab).

But there was the case of Natalie, Great Aunt Mary's only

child, a squat, dark girl with, according to my mother, "Indian blood" via her father from a nameless South American tribe. My mother's stories of Natalie depicted her as the family scapegoat. "'Oh mother, I'd rather die,'" Natalie wailed when her mother insisted she wear every one of her three winter coats so as to lighten her suitcase as they returned from a trip to her father's homeland.

After Dr. Andrade died, the family would never again order additions to their monogrammed Tiffany flatware and Limoge dinnerware. But appearances must be kept up, and it fell to Natalie to cull the lesser of the family possessions for Christmas presents for my grandmother, such as poultry shears with remains of a fowl still stuck to the blades, and a pair of desiccated men's suspenders (her father's?) which, when stretched out, stayed that way.

I saw the interior of Aunt Mary's 95th street house as a small child after she died. We stood in the first floor foyer; the smoke from my father and grandfather's cigarettes swirling in the shaft of sunlight between heavy window drapes. I couldn't read the funny papers splayed on the floor but I was fascinated by an object on the newel post at the bottom of the stairs: a plaster camel, draped in fringed and tasseled velvet, atop which sat a little turbaned black boy similarly dressed in velvet and holding in each hand a round white electric globe. This object suggested wealth which must have been in dwindling supply now that Natalie's father and mother were gone. Years later my mother interpreted for me: "The neighborhood was changing for the worse into Spanish Harlem." I pictured an elderly Nathalie sitting on her stoop with neighborhood women. "She says the neighbors steal from her but where else can she go? She speaks their language." A non English language, a language of the conquered, consigned her to poverty. "She was a throwback," my mother explained. "Not our blood."

4

A Child's Garden of Diversity

My town was, as I've said, mostly white and middle class and with only two immigrants that I remember: an Eastern Bloc family with the ailing child and a family of Estonians whose daughter, a tall, blond quiet girl, was in my class. But ordinary life could seem alien, outlandish.

In summer, when I had nothing to do, I was more likely to be aware of terrifying bits of nature. At dusk, insects increased their buzzing to an agonizing tinnitus level with the additional smacks of June bug carapaces hitting the screens, making my bedroom feel as if it were under attack. During the day, bugs flew around conjoined in lovemaking, snapping and rattling. Sometimes interspecies battles broke out as a bumblebee and a hawk moth would fall to the ground and tumble in a mad fit of buzzing to the death. Most agonizing to me were the locusts that began a hellish whirring in late June and reached daylong shrieking throughout August until some of them shed their outer shells on the bark of trees to continue life in another form. I shuddered lest I encounter one of their husks. But bugs were the least of my worries.

The Stamwitt's lived near the bottom of our street in a postwar bungalow with dark blue shutters into which had been cut crescent moons. I don't remember ever seeing Mr Stamwitt who must always have been at work. Mrs Stamwitt was the key player, a neat little woman in a dress and pumps who, as I rode up the sidewalk on my bike, a habit I maintained until age 8, when I was allowed to ride in the street, would appear at her front door and holler at me not to make tire tracks on her grass. This reprimand would cause me to pee in terror. Sometimes she would accost me if I was walking in such a way that she was convinced I was making tracks with my rain boots. "Right now!" she'd shout. "Or I'll call your mother!."

These days, children dismiss this kind of adult behavior as a sign that the person is "crazy" or "messed up" or "dumb." But in my era, or in my psyche, at least, Mrs Stamwitt's outbursts made her a species of witch and her evil signs were the moons cut into the shutters of her house. My brother Jim and I called her "the lady with the moons" and rather than cross to the other side of the street, we were drawn to the test of passing by her house. Years later I discovered that my mother and Mrs. Stamwitt were good friends and would spend hours 'gassing,' as my mother called it, on the phone. But unlike Mrs. Stamwitt, there were legitimate threats lurking in plain sight.

The Prentisses lived two houses down from us. They seemed "childless" as my mother said, but a daughter in her early twenties was away in what my mother termed "the ladies branch" of the army. I never saw Bubbles as she was called, but I understood that she was rising rapidly in the ranks.

Mrs. Prentiss was known for hanging out her wash earlier than any other woman on our street. Even as a child I wondered what made this act such a big deal. Wash pinned, she disappeared for the rest of the day, perhaps shopping or playing bridge. It was inconceivable to me that she joined the men on their trek to and from work. Mr. Prentiss, it appeared, did not work. I would see him on the glassed in side porch reading the newspaper. A small man in dark trousers and a white shirt, he resembled a male version of his wife in her trim black skirt and white blouse.

One summer afternoon, as I was walking down the street on locust patrol, Mr. Prentiss opened his front door and beckoned. He had a treat for me. Having never recovered from an aged aunt branding me as "stocky," I considered sweets the source of my desire and humiliation. I needed a treat.

The Prentiss's living room was papered and painted in shades of beige with a highly polished baby grand taking pride of place by a window. On top of the closed piano lid sat a crystal jar filled with crimson ribbon candy. I concentrated on the glowing candy that I imagined was cinnamon flavored. Mr. Prentiss opened the jar and held it out to me. I could have two pieces, one for each hand. I nearly blanched at the indulgence of this offer but eagerly accepted.

He sat down in a wing back chair. "Let's you and me talk." Although I was big for my age, he seemed to easily lift me under the arms and sit me on his lap. The candy was intensely sweet, not like cinnamon. I let the dissolved sugar run down my throat.

"I bet I can tell how old you are." He tightened his arms along the outsides of my legs.

I couldn't help crunching down on the center of one ribbon while the other one I tried to suck discreetly. My fingers were sticky.

"Let me think." His lap began going up and down.

One ribbon was nearly gone. I crunched it into a mass of sweet shards.

"You. Are." His lap gave a shudder. "You are getting to be." Shudder.

I went to work on the other piece of candy.

"Nine years old!" And his lap rode up again. I could feel him jiggling his thighs around a hard place.

"I want to go home." Mumbled through sugar slush. I slid off his lap.

"Oh sure! Sure you can!"

I looked at his face for the first time. Red as Santa.

"Take more!" He held out two more ribbons. I didn't want them but I took them.

"You're a good little girl!" Mr. Prentiss smiled like something was hurting him.

I was outside the door, down the sidewalk. I didn't thank him. I didn't say goodbye.

Many weeks later, when my mother and I were passing the Prentiss's house on our way to Saturday night Confession, I told her about how he went up and down. I don't remember her reaction but I said nothing more and soon forgot the incident until years later when I heard that Mr. Prentiss had called in the next door neighbor's daughter Muriel Bowker. He disappeared and came downstairs naked.

"'I suppose you want us to leave,'" Mrs. Prentiss was quoted as saying to Muriel's mother.

I don't know what happened to the Prentiss's. No police were called. I was in high school by then and had real boys to contend with.

5

Race Riot

Ada's brother, JB, brought Ada to our house to clean in the morning after we went to school. My father drove her home and I sometimes went with them.

Ada lived in Chairville, a tiny black town out toward the Pines. Her house sat up on cinder blocks. As far as I could see, it had a door but no windows. It was sided with tar paper and roofed with asphalt shingles. A black person in a black house with no windows.

"That's my Christmas tree," she told us, as we passed the winking red and green lights of the RCA radio towers. The implication was that she didn't have a Christmas tree but was grateful for this public display of light. I was seven years old. I didn't think radio towers were substitutes for Christmas. Was this Jim Crow? Was she telling us she was satisfied with poverty?

Ada had a tomcat named Stinkingale. His misbehaving and his smell were the subject of stories I wish I could remember.

This quiet Gullah woman treated me pleasantly but I don't remember any affection, any thought of including Ada at family parties the way I discovered later that middle class Jews sometimes did with their servants.

There were black men and women working in Rivertown but I didn't know them. There were no black people at the Catholic church my mother took us to each Sunday. There weren't any at dancing class or at the Country Club although my family didn't belong to the golf club either. My father had never had time or money for recreation beyond pool as a young man and monthly poker games later.

When we sailed our 14 foot Dusters in the Delaware River, there were no blacks at the historic but ramshackle Yacht Club, although there was a Jew who sailed a Celebrity which he "moored out," instead of hoisting back on the pier after each sail. He may not have lived in Rivertown. But another Jew did live in Rivertown, on Thomas Avenue, in a house I preferred to our own, having many French windows looking out on a garden with an arbor.

Black people lived on Penn Street, named for William Penn, a short street that ended at the Delaware River. The houses were late 19th century frame houses with front yards. By Rivertown standards they were shabby with chain link fences in front but now they are renovated and choice, and the atmosphere on Penn is genteel and leafy.

When I was in high school my mother inexplicably informed me that southern New Jersey was close—she seemed thrilled to tell me—to the Mason Dixon Line that separated North from South. In fact, some people believed that the southernmost tail of New Jersey in Cape May County actually fell below the line. Southern magnolia trees lined the streets of Cape May Court House just as they did in the deep south. Point of antebellum pride. The patrician south was what my mother was invoking although she had been only once, on the sit-up train to Atlanta, to visit my father in an Army hospital after WWII. She didn't like the food. Too greasy. Food was a dividing line. If a food or dish "did not agree" with her, my mother rejected the whole context in which it had been eaten: the day and season, the place and people. She verbally banished the world that caused the food to appear at her table.

Race riots: spoken by my mother and, while not specifically southern, it had something to do with black people, like grits. These riots were part of a conversation in the kitchen with my father in the evening with drinks. I was somewhere underfoot. She was dismissing some conflict among teenagers that took place at the shabby high school in the next town. Not our kind. But she never said that. Her tone was blasé, as if race riots were a fact of life I needed to know about so as better to avoid. Whites involved in such an event were no better than blacks, she seemed to say, people we shouldn't associate with. I imagined people running, dangerously fast and angry, because riot meant anger. It was happening near where I lived, but far enough away not to be a threat like the crash and boom of the dredges on the river. Soon I would learn that she had gone to this high school and that I would, too.

For a child, Rivertown in the 1950's was like a town in 5th century Italy but without chickens. Like ancient children, I'd never been farther than 5 miles in any direction from my house, except when my mother and I took the bus to Philadelphia or my father drove us the 40 miles to the seashore, a rare treat.

In Rivertown, anybody different stood out, for instance Harry Mills who carried the flag at the front of the Fourth of July parade. Harry was old and retarded. A colored man who worked at the coal yard. We could hear his glorious baritone as we passed on the way to school. Singing wasn't something common on the streets of Rivertown.

The bank was a good place to see odd people. A granite temple on Main Street. On Friday nights after dinner, my father would lead us like a group of pilgrims to worship at this altar of Mammon while he bought my brother and me a savings bond for our education. Sometimes we stood in line before the wicket of Muriel Janeway, a woman who wore mannish suits and short, slicked back hair. According to our mother, she lived with another woman and the neighbors could hear their fights but then they would make up and Muriel would bring home flowers from the florist shop in the next town. "She's the man," I overheard my mother explain to my father who snorted. Sometimes Pineys were in line, thin pale men and women with a kid or two straggling behind in old clothes. According to our mother, the family anthropologist, Pineys lived deep in the Pine Barrens and rarely came to town and their pale skin and thin pale hair and pink eyes showed they were inbred, possibly "feeble-minded" according to our father.

Arthur Miner came to our school in 4th grade. Arthur was the greatest nine- year-old athlete any of us had ever seen. He was quiet but not shy and he lived in a row house a block from the school. He could run, pitch, catch, jump, throw and hit a baseball as if he'd been practicing from the day he was born. I never spoke to him nor heard him speak, have no memory of his presence in class. But this: I saw what was under his black skin after he suffered a playground injury. I was part of the group of kids who leaned close to see the shock of wet crimson tissue beneath the torn black flesh. Arthur Miner was scouted in high school and awarded an athletic scholarship to a fine college. Much later I heard he was blinded in an industrial accident at his job the summer before he was to start classes.

6

Dentistry

When I was ten, a colored dentist moved to town. My parents could never have afforded to buy Dr. Brown's house on Main Street. Too big; expensive; too old; too good a location. My father moved into his father-in-law's house with my mother after the war. He took over his father-in-law's building business. His prized possession was his Ford.

My father, handsome, broad shouldered and dark haired, was raised in Iowa and upstate New York in the time of open farm land, a booming railroad bringing freight to the small towns along the Erie Lackawanna line. After his own father died, his mother sent two of his sisters to an orphanage and farmed out my father to a neighbor. My father dropped out of high school at seventeen to support the family and left town to work as a carpenter's helper.

"How did you get out of town?" I asked during one of his stories.

"You walked out." He voice was flat.

I could see him, on a sepia day in late fall, with a sack and a suitcase by the side of a dirt road.

My father was devoted to his cars all his life and to The Ford Motor Company as he called it, source of his first car, a Model A, and many cars thereafter until the Country Squire station wagon, each car a symbol of his dogged rise in status.

When we rode in one of his cars to visit his mother in the Southern Tier of New York State, near the scenes of his early manhood, my father would go back in time. Prone to storytelling as his means of communication, he would become silent.

On one of our hurried visits to my grandmother's bedside, we stopped at a restaurant somewhere in New York State. This was before the Country Squire, on the tailgate of which our mother fried ham and eggs or heated up baked beans for lunch by the roadside. We were in a smaller sedan and we stopped at what I could tell, from the slight curl of my father's lip, was a 'women's restaurant.' Blue and white wallpaper, pastel tablecloths, an elderly waitress in a white apron. This being Sunday, we ordered pot roast. To begin, the waitress brought us each a bowl of sliced apples and walnuts and celery in mayonnaise sauce. Waldorf salad. My father glared at this sweet appetizer as if someone had asked him to wear a dress. Then he began to speak:

"A colored man goes to the dentist to have a tooth extracted. The dentist tells the Negro to take off his trousers. The Negro asks why. The dentist says, 'because I'm going to remove the tooth—'"

"Jim," my mother said. "Jim."

"'through his'—" my father glanced at me.

"JIM!"

"'...through his backside.'" He chuckled, shot my mother a triumphant look.

"That's enough, Jim."

The joke baffled me anatomically but I knew it was violently cruel. Instead of condemning my father I felt sorry for him. Only ignorant, underprivileged people—my mother's words—thought a joke like that was funny, let alone would tell it to his family at a restaurant where the waitress served Waldorf salad as an appetizer, something my father said only homos—"panty waists"—ate. Maybe the joke was his revenge on the salad. The tooth joke was never mentioned again but it hammered home a fact: my father occupied a place of immunity from the standards my mother—a snob—applied to the rest of the world. He was not well educated or sophisticated. My mother had gone to four years of a Philadelphia art school. "Dear," she said to me years later when I was critical of a boyfriend she had indicated she favored. "You must take them as you find them."

"Is he one of us?" she would ask my father about someone new in town. Was this a game? I wondered. My mother's game to simulate my father's entry to the middle class? Apparently the tooth joke was not a deal breaker, just a moment of rural backwardness like the naked light bulb dangling from my grandmother's bedroom ceiling.

As I've mentioned, our mother did not drive, out of respect for my father's possessiveness about his vehicle. On rainy days he would drop us off at mass, "gas up" the car, buy the newspaper and park up the street, reading the paper, smoking and listening to gospel music. That glorious shouting escaping from the open car window along with his unfiltered Camel smoke sounded like compensation for his ignorance, yet he would never have played such music in our house where I had memorized the Victory at Sea records. Just as he listened to opera in his workshop but we never heard it in the house. Music carried him to worlds he secretly craved.

7

Penn Street

Once a week after school I walked along 4th Street to the Catholic Church for Catechism class. I discovered Penn Street where, as I mentioned earlier, the coloreds lived. One block long from 4th street to the Delaware River, Penn Street was named for William Penn, whom I was taught was the founder of Philadelphia and later learned was a Quaker. I knew about the Friends School in Moorestown and the Friends Cemetery with graves marked by modest white stones, like loaves of bread. Quakers practiced simplicity and humility, called each other "thee and thou" but saved their money, often became rich and lived in handsome old houses. Perhaps the street's name was meant to credit William Penn with benevolence towards black people of his Quaker brethren. Much later I learned that he owned slaves as many early Quakers did.

Occasionally I rode my bike down Penn Street on my way to

the river. I do not remember black people outside and it was only decades later that I saw the African Methodist Episcopal Church that stood midway down the block. There must have been people around but they were invisible to me. We were seeing what we wanted to see, what we had seen our parents see. *Get a nigger off the street.*

Get a white person off the street. That sentence means nothing. A nigger has no agency so he can be 'got.' You could do things with a black person that you couldn't do with a white person. Your grandfather could be his master, and your father the same. You didn't see your grandfather or father ever in the company of black people but you heard that they made use of black men for work. They got them off the street where, presumably, the black men were doing nothing.

So, by the time I road my bike down Penn Street, I wasn't intending to see people the way I saw people on Elm Street, what my mother referred to as Our Street. I wasn't expecting to see houses like the one we lived in although the houses on Penn were more venerable than ours. Were the houses scarred and messy? Were the yards cluttered with bikes and toys and junk? Or is that a hangover from media images with no direct connection that street?

Nobody said *the dark side of town*. Nobody said *Darkies*. None of these archaisms were spoken because they didn't need to be. Darkies. It would have been shocking to see black people as real, just as I was shocked, on the school playground, to see the pink flesh and crimson blood inside the gash on Arthur Miner's leg, so similar to my own.

In this way, black men were invisible in their own world but they worked for whites. Just as black women like Ada Bryant, our cleaning lady, worked for us but she wasn't one of us.

What I knew about Ada I was told by my mother: names, places, phrases, adages.

"'He's little but he's loud'" my mother told me Ada said of my brother as a baby.

"'The longer you live, the longer you live.'" Ada's maxim about the inscrutable and ongoing nature of experience. That adage may have been told to me as comfort after I broke up with a boyfriend.

There were no black people in Our Church, as my mother called the Catholic church, and none at the ochre tiled Parochial School across the street.

"What is your background?" a nun demanded of my brother when he made a mistake in Catechism class.

"Scottish and Irish."

"Ah!" she glared in triumph. "A bad mixture."

It was so easy to be the wrong kind of person even if you were white.

8

Shine

We've finished dinner and my mother is washing dishes. I'm standing in the kitchen doorway, looking into the hall where my father is sitting in one of the two side chairs that are kept there and that nobody uses. In front of him kneels a black man in dark trousers and a short sleeve shirt. This is Ben Deacon, the only black person I've seen in our house besides Ada, the cleaning woman. He sells Knapp shoes. These are the only shoes my father can wear, he says, because they don't hurt his bunions. Being in our front hallway isn't the same thing as being in the living room. Deliverymen can stand at the front door and step through the doorway with a sheave of my father's dry-cleaned suits or two dozen eggs. Ben has come farther into our hallway than the man from the cleaners. I know why Ben Deacon is in our hall but his presence unsettles me.

Ben kneels in front of my father and unties his old shoes

and slips them off to show my father's dark blue socks. I've only seen my father's bare feet once, at the seashore. They are pale and hairless, a sharp contrast to the rest of his body. My father's hands are strong, hairy, sun tanned. His feet are weak, hairless, as defenseless as a shelled mollusk. They embarrass me. In our house, only little kids show their feet.

Ben expertly slides my father's foot into a shoe and laces it up, picks up the left shoe and slides my father's foot into it with the help of a silver shoe horn. He laces the shoe, sits back. "How's that?" My father stands up, shifts his weight, takes a step. "Dandy," he says. "I don't know what this outfit does, but they always seem to fit me perfectly." Ben chuckles. "That's why I sell them."

While Ben slides off the new shoes, my father makes a date to see him next spring for a pair of air cooled, side mesh oxfords. Ben places the new shoes between tissue paper in their box. My father sits down again while Ben fits the old shoes back on my father's feet and laces them while my father watches him with a pleasant expression that is almost a smile.

9

Home Schooling

One of my father's remote elderly relatives, Cousin Virgil, a widower from Iowa, came east on his honeymoon to show off his new wife, Naomi. Cousin Virgil had a pacemaker to keep his heart beating. My father said he was very lucky that this tiny machine had just been invented otherwise he'd be dead. But Virgil's greater luck was in his choice of a wife.

"My God can you believe it?" my father said over a hastily consumed gin and tonic before they arrived—the newlyweds did not drink. "A virgin. Virgil found himself a sixty-three-year-old virgin." I knew about the Virgin Mary but I assumed Cousin Naomi was a Baptist. My father had had been raised Baptist, dunked in an Iowa creek and as a result loathed all religion.

These elderly cousins presented themselves at the front screen door. I heard my mother's welcoming warble, emitted at moments of social anxiety. I came running into the hall eager to witness the source of her upset.

Cousin Virgil was a short plump man in plaid trousers and a short-sleeved shirt. His wife, skinny with a hatchet profile and gray hair in a braid coiled around her head, stood at least six inches taller than her new husband.

Guests never brought gifts, but Cousin Naomi held out a bunch of violets.

"Oh, how precious! How darling!" My mother accepted the violets and found a recently used shot glass to contain them. Our yard was covered with violets that eventually someone would mow. She placed the violets in the middle of the dining room table.

Our guests asked for glasses of water, which I brought them as they sat in the living room with my father. I envied my athletic brother his dispensation at baseball practice.

This being high summer, my mother had made boiled tongue which she served chilled with raisin sauce and asparagus, which Jim and I had recently picked. ("Snap it off right at the ground!" my father commanded. "Waste not want not.")

Back in the kitchen, my mother showed me how to use the device that created riced boiled potatoes by squeezing them through holes to emerge as tiny white worms.

We settled ourselves around the dining room table. My father was in the act of forking tongue onto a plate when Cousin Virgil rose from his chair to say a long-winded grace that named every member of our family, including Jim on the Little League pitcher's mound.

While Cousin Virgil discussed life insurance with my father, I concentrated on the lace collar on Cousin Naomi's dress. She had tatted it with leftovers from their wedding coverlet. She smiled as she said this and patted Cousin Virgil's hand. Her face powder had settled into the creases on her forehead and around her mouth.

After dinner, as the house temperature crested at 89 degrees, my father led his cousins to aluminum lawn chairs under the sycamore in the backyard. Uncle Virgil disappeared and amazed me be returning, nearly naked, in blue bathing trunks. Without a word, he opened the chain link fence around our little concrete pool and dove in. Cousin Naomi squealed.

Once they were back in their car and on their way to Atlantic City, my mother assessed the newlyweds: "He went all through the forest and came out with a crooked stick."

"Oh, I don't know." My father chuckled. "A long skinny plank makes the best teeter."

"Jim!" My mother chuckled.

There must have been homes in which parents felt responsible for imparting ethics, morals, *doing the right thing* or, as we say now, *leading by* example, but our house was not one of them. While my father occasionally entertained us with barnyard witticisms, our Mother was the chief interpreter of the outside world through nasty adages and little poison pills of social comment.

Sputnik was her name for the little Eastern European boy with a hole in his heart whose family lived at the bottom of our street. Across the street lived Jerry Hannah one grade ahead of us with a speech impediment. My mother called him Jay Jay Ha Ha. "Me think him sick in bed," Jay explained when I asked about his brother. Family hilarity ensued and the phrase became a well-worn joke when any of us were sick.

Mrs. Ellersby, an unusually fat woman for those times, waddled up to our house one summer afternoon with the rolling gate of a painfully arthritic hip. A Republican County Committee member, Mrs. Ellersby must have been bringing my mother campaign literature. I was arranging flowers on the hall table.

We watched Mrs. Ellersby make her way, panting, back to her car.

"Next size comes on wheels," stated Mom, the funniest woman in the world.

Cousin Jackie, my father's niece, was always fast. Too many boyfriends, too many late nights, car rides, necking. This I overheard my mother discussing with my father's other sister, not Jackie's mom who was also "no bargain." Jackie got knocked up in high school, had to get married.

"They were playing around on the outside," my mother explained.

I was terrified. Outside of your body, outside the tickling blemish between your legs? I had never been told about sex but I imagined the stuff—I hadn't yet heard of sperm—crawled into her, possibly through a man's gabardine trousers and her underpants.

"The doctor had to perform the rabbit test."

Rabbit? He pulled it out of a hat? No, the rabbit was given something taken from Jackie, maybe some of her blood. It died. Proof that she was pregnant.

These scanty details stewed for weeks in my caldron of worries. The body and its substances could turn on you at any moment. An old man up the street had lung cancer, which I heard as thumb cancer, confirming my fears about a tiny bump on my hand.

The year after the rabbit test, Jackie and her new husband, Danny, came to visit. My mother had bought Jackie nylons and a garter belt to wear under her wedding dress since Jackie's mother was off somewhere with a new boyfriend, a man with a foot fetish, my mother explained. My father had given Jackie twenty dollars for the honeymoon.

We're in the stifling living room. Jackie wears pedal pushers, with hems cut zigzag like elf pants. The baby is not around. I'm fascinated by Danny's black hair combed in a single wave off his forehead and his short sleeve shirt with cuffs rolled once. Jackie and Danny are the only teenagers who have ever visited.

That evening, I'm in the kitchen as my mother fries tomatoes and recaps the visit for my father. What did she think of Danny? My father wants to know.

"A wet smack," says Mother. "Mr. Sent For and Couldn't Come."

10

Belle

Just to refresh your memory: Belle Brown, the first upper-middle-class colored girl to come to our school. Sixth grade. Only child. Her father was a dentist. They lived in a big white Victorian on Main Street with a wrap-around porch.

Mrs. Bush, the old white lady across the street comes out on her porch.

"Boy. When you finish mowing over there, would you come do our lawn?" She assumes that a black man with a lawn mower must be somebody's help.

Doctor Brown obliges, mows her lawn. The story flies around town, appalling, hilarious, shameful.

Belle was smart and better dressed than any girl in our class. It never occurred to me that we could be friends but I admired her from my desk in the next row.

I don't remember her being aloof but neither do I remember

her being chatty. Why would this girl want to make friends with a bunch of little white girls in a town where people treated her father like a servant?

Later, she went to Friends School, the high school I longed to attend but could not afford, in Moorestown, the rich Quaker town five miles away. I never saw her again. Her prominent, bronze profile like a Native American. Her smooth brown calves, so much slimmer than mine, with soft ankle socks and Weejuns, the loafers I wanted but were too costly. Pleated tartan skirts and demur cardigans. She dressed like a college girl. I was never invited to her house and it never occurred to me to ask her to one of our basement parties.

Much later I heard from someone on a trip back to Rivertown that Belle had researched the African American community on Penn Street and the African Methodist Episcopal Church that anchored that street and still does. I have searched for Belle Brown on the Internet but have found nothing.

11

Names

Another family named Brown moved to our town in the late 1950's. The Browns had the same name as Dr. Brown but instead of being colored they were Jewish, which made them socially halfway between white and black. How did I know they were Jewish? It must have come up at the dinner table like most things, or I could have overheard it in the kitchen. "That's not the original name," my mother would have explained to my father. The Browns lived in a former carriage house a block from the river. I never saw Mr. and Mrs. Brown at close enough range to remember their faces but I did notice what they drove—a woody station wagon—and the color they repainted their house— grey green, a new color in houses and decorating. My friend Connie's mother explained the particular shade of green as sage, and how it was going to be an important color when it caught on.

They had no children, unusual for our town. Most people

without children were old or somehow marked by misfortune. They couldn't have children, a scar on their marriage. But the Jewish Browns didn't seem diminished. The house was empty during the weekdays and lively with dinner parties on weekends. Sometimes both Browns worked outside planting shrubs and small trees that bloomed gorgeously in spring. They owned a patio beneath an arbor of wisteria where I once saw them sitting with friends. The Browns, I concluded, were ahead of their time.

There were no Jews in our school, no synagogue in our town, no Jews at the golf club. One had joined the yacht club but lived across the river. Sol Solberg, the Jewish sailor with the teak-decked sailboat, was a dentist. He sometimes sailed in free for all races but most of the time when I rode my bike along the river bank, I saw Sol Solberg's boat moored in exile slightly upriver from the yacht club.

Felicity Eck was in my first-grade class. She was an only child with long black ringlets. She actually wore a hoop skirt under her dresses and slept in a canopy bed and when she was 12 her parents built the town's first 20 by 40 foot in ground swimming pool. I envied her special doll-like porcelain status. Her father owned a jewelry store where my mother got my father's watch repaired.

"It used to be Eckstein," my friend Connie told me. "They changed it."

Jan Jervis lived on our street and was in my class. Her sister Gail danced with colored girls along the chain link fence outside of high school. Wild Gail copying the colored girls. Nigger lover somebody said, a not uncommon term. Gail who got pregnant by Denny, a skinny white guy with a black duck's ass hair do. They had to get married, lived in an apartment over the hardware store.

Jan and I visited Gail one spring evening. She took us in the baby's room. The shades were drawn, a nightlight made the room glow pink, claustrophobic, a stifling womb. Gail was even shorter than Jan but she made up for it with tits and ass as my brother said. She stood on tippy toes, leaned into the crib to pick up a tiny pink blob. Eyes tight shut, it nuzzled into her shoulder, snorting.

"Oh, she's so cuuuuute," Jan whispered. I said nothing, couldn't wait to get out of there, had no feeling for babies and was terrified of getting pregnant, since I believed that sperm could crawl through underwear. I can't blame my sex notions on the Catechism nuns. I'd always been the one in the family with the active imagination. "High strung," my grandfather said.

My mother hated her pregnancy with twins. Siamese twins were in the news and she was sure she was carrying conjoined fetuses. "Don't worry," her obstetrician said. "If that is the case, you will never see them." She was nearly 40 when we were born and her doctor anaesthetized her for the high forceps delivery, from which I still bear scars.

I felt sorry for Gail. When we were out on the street, I asked where Denny was.

"Night shift," Jan said. "They do a lot of joking around. You know. To make it fun."

Make what fun?

"Last night they had a mashed potato fight at dinner."

Fun in an apartment above a hardware store with shades

down to keep out the heat and noise. I'd never had sex and had only just learned what 'rape' meant, but I didn't hold out hope for this marriage or the future of the baby whose name I had forgot to ask.

"Mercy," Jan informed me.

12

Conservative

I don't remember, at age 3, being taught to shout "Hip Hurrah for Tom Dewey," as I am told I did, but I do remember liking Ike for winning the war and giving reassuringly dull speeches.

The Kennedy/Nixon campaign stands out vividly as a period of high excitement in our household since my mother was by then president of the Republican County Committee and deep into pamphlet folding parties, solicitations and phone calls.

Democrats were the source of all impediments to freedom if not the source of evil. My mother reserved her greatest rancor for the woman who worked in the Rivertown post office. *That damned Democrat* or when she'd had an especially frustrating day, *that Democrat bitch.* Years later, when I was doing my own bulk mailings for nonprofits, I realized that my mother probably needed someone to blame for her difficulties figuring out the intricacies of mass mailings. At the time I was baffled that this polite, soft spoken woman I'd seen behind the post office counter could transform into a demon.

My mother's struggles with the U.S. Postal Service were nothing compared to her catastrophic response to Kennedy's win. I was dressing for high school on the day after the election when full-throated blubbering erupted from my parents' bedroom. My father had long since gone to work. My mother lay sprawled, fully dressed across their unmade bed, lamenting. *I cannot go on. After all our hard work. Those fiends!* etc.

My grandfather emerged from his bedroom and came to stand in the doorway, jingling the change in his pocket. A devout Catholic whose parents had emigrated from Ireland, he had broken ranks to vote for Kennedy.

Sensing her father's presence, my mother got up on one elbow. "How could you?" she sobbed. "Do you see, now, what you've done, siding with them?"

What had he done? Kennedy was cool. I was glad he'd won.

I went back to my room to spray my flip. I didn't want to be late for school.

I knew there was something the matter with my parents' politics but I didn't know what it was. The chain link fence around our swimming pool was an eyesore but I didn't understand why my father blamed its existence on the Democrats, and even so, wasn't it a good idea to keep little neighbor kids from falling in and drowning? In later decades, my father blamed Democrats for his difficulties opening pill bottle lids. He was disappointed when I couldn't find him lead paint in Canada, where I had moved, to paint his barn. *Damned welfare state.*

Both my parents believed in being "public spirited," as my

mother called taking part in town affairs. I admired their work on behalf of the planning board, town council and school board while most other parents I knew spent their evenings playing bridge or watching TV.

But Democrats lurked on these committees and sometimes "plagued" my mother, as when "that Harpwell woman won't stop plaguing me about the sewer ordinance." Hysterics could break out at night, in my parent's bedroom, for example, when, at town council, my father cast the deciding vote against fluoridation. What's wrong with Fluoride? I wondered. Keeps kids from getting cavities.

"They'll pillory him!" my mother sobbed. "And all because he doesn't think the town has enough information." In truth, I sensed that my father had heard the rumor that fluoride was poison, a Communist plot.

"Come the revolution!" he would say after his second rye and soda. What revolution? Where?

I was better able to parse my mother's euphoric comment at a dinner party: "Jim likes to say that we're somewhere to the right of Barry Goldwater."

I cringed. By that time I was in college and part of a crowd that booed this presidential candidate when he made a campaign stop.

Much later, I came to understand my father's hatred of Democrats as a twisted envy of FDR's New Deal. He had come of age before social security, had been farmed out to support his six siblings and widowed mother, had left high school to find full-time work. No one helped him, yet he survived with an abiding bitterness for government programs that came later. Most undeserving among destitute people were blacks.

Even in rural retirement in largely white New England, my father held his racism close. Case in point: the snowy night one Christmas when a car swerved around the curve in front of our house and landed in the front yard. The untrammeled golden retriever Rusty barked the alarm and my parents came downstairs. A black man stood at the back door. My father opened the inside door but kept the storm door on latch as the man explained that he skidded on a patch of ice.

"There's ice out there, that's for sure," my father said. The man thought he could back his car down onto the road, but if not, could he use their phone to call a tow truck. I knew my father had a tractor and a come-along in the barn, but he did not offer it. My parents watched through the kitchen window as the man slowly backed onto the road, gave a brief toot of the horn and continued on his way. Perhaps in response to the horn, Rusty began frantic barking.

"You never have liked black people, have you, boy?" My father ruffled Rusty's ears.

After my father died, my mother, who had never lived one day alone in her life, settled into a long, productive old age. Her political and social views softened now that she didn't need to protect her husband's bitterness and fear.

"Oh, my Lord in heaven, I have never seen such a beautiful man!" she said, of OJ Simpson's *New Yorker* photo in that LA courtroom. My mother was an artist. Guilt or innocence was trumped by beauty.

She accepted abortion rights and made friends with some local back to the landers and a gay couple who ran an antique shop and came to her dinner parties. She never abandoned her beloved Republicans but her loyalty was stretched thin when Evangelicals and the Far Right ascended and she nearly voted for Clinton. I wish she had lived to see Obama.

13

Snow Day

Late afternoon of what must have been a snow day, a rarity in South Jersey, I'm standing at the top of Our Street, the steep part that ends at Highway, a name in ancient times to designate the highest, most open path. Now Highway borders the south side of the town's private golf course. Children sledded on the golf links when there was enough snow, which was rare. We wore the links down to the grass with the metal runners of our Flexible Flyers. We were trespassing but nobody drove us off.

I'm with my friend Patty, short for Patience. Patty is a Quaker, a faith I, as a Catholic, envy for its suggestion of pious wealth and the many leaded windows of brick private schools. No matter that, according to my mother, Patty's mother used to be an Episcopalian. I envy Patty. Tall and lean with high cheekbones and blond hair that she is brave enough to wear in an old fashioned braid down her back.

We've spent the afternoon sledding and now we're taking a few rides down the steep part of Our Street. A late January afternoon. Lights are coming on in the living rooms and kitchens and on the porches of the Victorian houses along Highway. I've never been in any of these houses but I know the names of the people who live in some of them: the Fletchers, the Ballantines, the Driscolls. A black Lincoln comes along, chains clicking in the slush, turns into a driveway and parks under a portico. The driver's door opens and a woman gets out. I don't know her. Fur coat and slim legs in ankle boots. Mrs. Driscoll coming home from bridge, maybe.

I'm so lost in imagining her world that I don't realize Patty has disappeared, slid to the bottom of the steep part. She's getting off her sled, beckoning to me. I don't see the trio of figures coming from the other side of Highway. I take a running start and belly flop on to my sled and I'm swerving downhill, runners shedding sparks off the icy grit until I wipe out on a bare patch of macadam. Patty helps me up, brushes snow and cinders from the back of my jacket and corduroys. It's nearly dark but we'll take one more sled to the bottom of the steep part, then walk down to my house.

Three colored girls are at the top of our street. They don't have sleds but they stand like they're waiting for us.

"Who are they?" I ask Patty.

"I don't know. Do you know?"

"Of course I don't know."

There is one colored girl in school, so these girls must come from outside town. A fat girl with a red car coat; a short very black girl in a windbreaker and a medium girl with a long white scarf wrapped around and around her neck.

"Hey girl!"

Who are they talking to?

"Yeah, GIRL. YOU! What you doing, rolling around in the gutter."

"Yeah, she rolling in the gutter."

They're talking to me, not Patty. I glance at Patty. *HELP ME,*

Patty has a look on her face I've never seen before, a goofy smile. She's playing clown.

"Girl where you get those sleds?" Red coat.

"Yeah, I need me one a dem sleds." Windbreaker.

"From the hardware store." I begin walking downhill.

"No, right now!" White scarf.

"Yeah, let's take a sled ride."

"Yeah." The three girls begin walking downhill beside us.

"Gimme that sled!" This from the shortest girl who has been silent.

The other two girls skip, leap toward me and I jump back.

The three shriek. "She scared!"

"Bullies!" Patty intervenes, a blond war goddess. "We're going home and you should too!" A command.

"Oh yeah?" from the tall one in the white scarf. "Well guess what?'

"I don't care what!" Patty yelled. "Get outta here!"

"Oooo, she mad!" Red coat.

We're gaining speed, nearly at a run, sleds held close as if we still might belly flop one last time.

Suddenly the girls stop following us. They turn back up the hill.

"Your mom's a whore!" one of them screams.

Patty begins to fake cry, big loud blubbers meant to be heard up and down the street.

We're at my house, home safe. The girls have disappeared. No, Patty can't stay for dinner, she must go home and make icing for her mom's birthday cake.

Did we hug each other? Girls didn't. I don't recall us ever mentioning the sledding scene again.

14

Peach Street

For the mother of my best friend Connie, taste was a moral issue and morals bled into race.

Yeah, Creole babies with flashin' eyes softly whisper with tender sighs
And then you stop!
Oh won't you give your lady fair a little smile?
And then you stop!
You bet your life you'll linger there a little while
Yeah, there is heaven right here on earth with those beautiful queens
Yeah, way down yonder in New Orleans
Whoo!

We're listening to Freddie Cannon on WIBG AM radio, Philly, up in Connie's bedroom in 1959. Connie's mother calls us downstairs for Hawaiian punch and pretzels, a treat I would never have been allowed at home.

"Girls," she settles herself on the loveseat across from the couch where we sit looking out the picture window at the street. "Way Down Yonder in New Orleans!" she croons a thin soprano. "That's not a very nice song."

Connie and I stare at each other.

"Girls, do you know what 'creole' means?"

We don't. The South. Uncle Ben? Lil Abner? I'm staring at a collection of blue and white plates displayed on the wall, a crystal bowl, blue glass coasters on which sit our glasses of punch, the basket of pretzel sticks. I'd like to grab a fistful but that would not be polite.

"Girls, bad things are happening down South."

I've seen the National Guard on TV. I'm not interested. Eighth grade graduation is coming up and I'm making a speech about Culture, a new word, and my hair doesn't look good and the dress my mother made makes me look fat.

Mrs. Toms, the English teacher, changes the title of my speech to 'Our Creed," a word I've used only to recite "The Apostles Creed" in Confirmation class. Mrs. Toms says it means "Belief." I don't know what I believe.

"Girls," Connie's mother says gently. "Creole means part white and part colored."

Maybe if I can find a piece of green velvet ribbon for a cummerbund.

"And that mixing is not good."

I have enough allowance money to go to the fabric store.

"Mixing what?" Connie is doing her duty, holding up her end of the conversation.

"The mixing of the races, black and white." Connie's mother

glares at us meaningfully. "That's why there's so much trouble down there." She brushes at her skirt. "You girls are going to high school next year and it's a different place. Not like Rivertown." She glances outside. Maybe a piece of that different place is creeping up on the house.

"May I please have some more punch?" Connie is the most polite of my friends.

When we went to college—me to Vermont and Connie to Delaware—the unthinkable occurred. Connie drew a black roommate. This fact was relayed to me by my mother at Christmas vacation. She must have found out through the information channels of Rivertown. She wasn't close friends with Connie's mother. I do not remember the two women ever being in each other's houses.

This situation must have been revealed the day Connie was driven to college by her parents. If the roommate had yet to arrive, Connie may have been left to face her. I imagine a tall girl—she would play varsity basketball—with stiffly straightened hair curled under in a pageboy, pink Bermuda shorts and a white blouse, white sneakers. An American Tourister suitcase similar to Connie's. Tall father and a plump mother in a pale blue dress and matching pumps. But Connie is too disoriented to see them clearly. They are three coloreds in her bedroom, her refuge in this new world.

"Good afternoon," says the mother.

Connie cannot speak. The daughter—until now only a name on a paper sent to her—from Little Falls, West Virginia, wherever that is.

The girl unsnaps the clips on the American Tourister.

Connie escapes from the room without a word, runs down the hall into the communal bathroom. Tears. Then a rush downstairs to the telephone. Her parents have not yet returned home. Mother is herself drying tears as they cross into New Jersey. Our baby is gone. Mom who went no farther than high school.

Connie must face the unimaginable: spending a night in a room with a colored person. She can't return to the room where her underwear and sweaters are folded in 'her' bureau, her blouses and skirts hung up in her closet, where her belongings are even now exposed to this contamination, for that is what it feels like. Creole ladies with flashing eyes.

What to do? She runs down the stairwell through the vestibule still full of chattering girls and parents lugging boxes, bags.

The sharp-eyed housemother is by her side, a hand on her arm. "Can I help you, dear?" She is experienced with girls unstrung by their first moments away from home. Some are more sheltered than others. Provide reassurance.

"I'm going to be sick."

The housemother leads her to a private bathroom. When Connie emerges, she finds the housemother and, sobbing, whispers her story.

"If your parents call Student Housing, they can arrange a room change."

Now, right now.

Housemother looks at her watch. "They won't be open until tomorrow morning."

Connie sobs. "I need to change now."

"We can get you all taken care of tomorrow morning." The

housemother needs to attend to a line of girls who are blissfully ignorant of Connie's impossible dilemma.

When Connie returns to her room, the colored people are gone. Maybe there was a mistake but here sits the suitcase on the other bed.

An emergency call from Connie's father to the housemother. We didn't pay for our daughter to come all the way to your college in order to be forced to live with a colored girl. There's no reason for it. Must be changed immediately.

Connie spends the night rolled up in her bed sheet, face to the wall. At dawn, the shape in the other bed is still sleeping while Connie packs her bag. She sits in the housemother's office until it opens.

The change is made. My mother delivers the news without comment and I never mention it to Connie. How would I have been in a similar situation? Perhaps more muted but, nonetheless, with shock and discomfort. In 1964, integration of formerly all white colleges was brand new. By the end of her freshman year Connie meets the man she will marry and she changes to a junior college near his home town.

15

PHS

The summer before I went to Pottsboro High School, a disgruntled white boy who hadn't made the varsity basketball team burned the place down, or as much as would burn before the fire department arrived, which was enough to require the school, when it opened in September, to run on split shifts: from 7:00 AM to noon and from noon to 7:00 PM, while construction pounded on the new addition.

The misery of my freshman year was a mix of repugnance and fear. 1960 was a fairly calm, prosperous time in South Jersey, but I rejected Pottsboro just as my mother had. She, too, had gone to the high school and she remembered murals being drawn by artists employed by the WPA. Murals of muscular men and women entering the various "walks" of life: manufacturing (smoke stacks, molten steel), business (desks, stenography pads), agriculture (tractors), building (architectural plans, rulers), education (mortar boards, lecterns), medicine (white coats), family life (babes in arms) and home economics (women in aprons with measuring cups). I stared at the murals without recognition during the chaos of changing classes. I knew they were intended to inspire us but, like most inspirational art, they seemed dead, from another time. They showed us a kinetic world of heroism while the stuffy halls of PHS smelled of boredom and despair.

My 7 AM homeroom class belonged to Mr Kohlbal, tall, loud mouthed, with black heads on his nose. He yelled out the roster: Flowers, Fink, Hill, Ianucci, Jimston, Kellerman! Kirby! Kirschner! How did I know that this was a Jewish name? Sheila Kirschner cowered at her seat opposite George Flowers in the next row, a tall, wise-cracking black boy tipping back in his chair, source of humor and life.

When, after weeks of yelling, "Don't be dumb all your life!" "Take a zero!" Kohlbal referred to him as a "mouthy nigger," George shot to his feet, strode to the door. The class was riveted. "You done it this time Cool Ball. I'm reporting YOU to the principal."

George Flowers, class hero. An entertainer, smarter than the teacher and with a limit to how much abuse he'd take, unlike white kids like me.

There were black girls I never spoke to, whose names I didn't know, the girls my friend Jan's sister danced with to learn the new steps. Their heads bobbed in unison. This was before portable radios, before boom boxes, cell phones. In winter they danced with their coats open, showing flashes of pastel sweaters.

I stood with a clutch of white kids on the other side of the black top. At the bell, we began to move toward the back entry.

The black girls kept dancing by the chain link fence, switching their legs in unison. I shot apprehensive glances at their skirts, tight over high, round backsides. *Creole ladies with flashing eyes.* They ignored us, laughed high notes that sounded like songs.

PHS looked like a chain link-surrounded prison and the basement was its dungeon. Health class took place in the dungeon. Health class taught you how your body got itself pregnant but it didn't teach you how not to get pregnant. Based on the quizzes we took each week, Enid Bailey, a colored girl, should have gotten an A+. She had experienced the insertion of the penis into the vagina and the ejaculation of spermatozoa against her cervix and into her uterus and its penetration of an ovum that had been released from the ovary into the fallopian tube and then the uterus. Sperm lived for 48 hours in the womb.

Enid did not identify the ejaculator. She didn't speak at all. She sat in a starched white blouse over a black skirt. Her straightened hair was raked back in in shock, as if caught in a high wind. Perhaps Enid didn't know the father. Perhaps someone jumped on her in an alley the way we'd been told rape happened. She was enduring her punishment quietly. She didn't dance by the chain link fence.

It seemed inevitable that my first experience of an unwed mother should be a black girl who, in my perception, had no feelings, no thoughts, no public words for what had happened to her.

The teacher, Miss Dankin, was the gym teacher and a lesbian. How did we know she was a lesbian in 1961? Everybody knew everything. Nobody wanted to talk about school but everybody wanted to talk about what happened at school. Everyone was watching everyone, figuring stuff out, judging, drawing conclusions, like the conclusion that Enid didn't have a boyfriend who was the father of her child.

A lesbian wasn't an outcast, like an unwed mother. A lesbian was just a woman who palled around with other women and liked women's sports. Miss Dankin didn't laugh or make eye contact with the class. She drew chalk diagrams of the male and female reproductive systems. She called on us to approach the blackboard and label the organs. She didn't call on Enid.

"Knock it off!" she'd yell at gossipers. "This is no joke!"

In that she was correct.

Later in high school, I got to know two black girls, June and Marilyn, both cheerleaders and good students. While June and I changed for gym, June talked about Barry, her boyfriend who lived in Philly, was going to Temple and who she planned to marry. June wore her hair in a perfectly pony tail like Jane Fonda. She could do splits and cart wheels. She had short muscular legs and big breasts and she wore cardigan sweaters over pleated skirts. Barry had already given her a ring with her birthstone, topaz, which she wore on her right hand. Every day I listened to the latest chapter in the story of Barry and June.

Marilyn and I were on the student council. I sat with her on a bus trip to a student government day, sat together in the auditorium while a school administrator talked about student government. To kill the boredom, Marilyn kept a tally of the times he paused.

"Fifty-seven uhs," she said, flatly, as the man left the stage.

I was flattered that Marilyn would sit with me and make a joke.

I was amazed at how normal Marilyn and June seemed. Normal meant like white people.

Scene with Mrs. Prince:

My Aunt Matty comes home from work. She is a first-grade teacher at the Spring Elementary School in Pottsboro. June's mother, Mrs. Prince, is cleaning house for her.

Aunt Matty hears the sound of her vacuum cleaner. She enters the living room to find June Prince's mother vacuuming while one of her young daughters does homework at Aunt Matty's dining room table. June Prince's mother looks up from her work and waves above the noise.

Aunt Matty goes to the freshly cleaned kitchen. She leaves her pocket book in its place on a chair by the bedroom door; she smells the aggressive sweetness of bathroom cleaner. June Prince's mother has too free of a hand with Aunt Matty's cleaning products.

She glances into the bedroom and receives a shock. A black infant is sleeping in the middle of the bed. She looks out a window. June Prince's mother's little son is sitting on the back step, petting Aunt Matty's usually aggressive German shepherd, Rudy. Aunt Matty is briefly charmed by this sight, but returns to feeling discomfited, threatened. Her house has been invaded.

She confronts June Prince's mother by the utility closet where she is returning the vacuum. A short woman, Aunt Matty rises up on her Naturalizers, folds her hands in a teacherly pose.

"I told her 'I'm not running a nursery,'" Aunt Matty took a sip from her rye and soda.

"Ada would say that woman was being 'dicty.'" My mother was slicing apples into a pie shell.

"What's 'dicty?'" I asked

"Being too high and mighty. Dictatorial. "

It seemed to me like Aunt Matty was dictating

June Prince's mother was a member of the NAACP, Aunt Matty said. That explained her letting her kids do their homework at her cleaning client's dining room table. I said the words in my head. *for the advancement of colored people.* People like Ada. Did June Prince's mother need to be advanced?

"I've been slaving all morning!" my mother would say. "Don't loll up there in bed while I'm slaving. Help!" "I'm a second class citizen. I'm just an unpaid worker in this house!"

Who was a slave? Someone who had work imposed on them against their will, who was not paid. Who exactly were slaves? I didn't think about it, didn't know, wasn't taught in school. What was the Civil War? A battle for states' rights. Why did the South want to secede? Wanted their own country. Why? Plantations and hoop skirts and cotton and servants. The Boll Weevil was a song about a bug Way Down upon the Sewanee River at the Darktown Strutters Ball. The North won the Civil War because we were smarter was what it came down to or, if not, I never learned why.

Sammy Boyd was the only black boy who ever entered our house. I see him sitting on the itchy living room couch between two other kids for a yearbook meeting. 1964. A sweet guy, mellow voice, easy laugh inside and outside of school.

How did I feel about Sammy being in our house? Self-conscious, uneasy, as if at any moment an adult might enter the room and tell him to leave or one of us white kids might say the kind of things they said among themselves or start trying to imitate the way a colored person talked. Just for fun. Because colored people said things in cool ways. That was a compliment to the colored person, right?

Uh...what's a fortification?

Well...uh...two twentifications.

Decades later, I would run into Sammy, now Samuel, in a bar in Montreal.

"Jimmy Morton's sister!" he laughed, looking up at me from a table of friends. He and my brother had played freshman football.

I was grateful he spoke to me first because I wasn't sure I was seeing the Sammy of my memory or a generic version of him *because didn't whites think all blacks look alike?*

16

Going South

A bus trip to Washington, DC was as far south as I'd ever been until my brother and I went to a regatta on the Chesapeake.

"Oh look! Boxwood!" my mother bent over a low hedge in front of our motel. "Oh! The scent!"

"Like cat pee," my brother said.

We were slightly below the Mason Dixon line and, according to my mother, everything would be different. People would be gentler and more polite and you'd be called ma'am. People's names would sound like what my mother called 'old money' and generations of landed gentry.

Is that why I let a boy named Leland Kingsman finger fuck me in the so-called playroom of his parents' house overlooking the bay while the adults were gathered at the yacht club?

The next day he avoids me. After the race I approach him on

the lawn in front of the yacht club where he's joking with his friends.

"Do you have a cigarette?" I plead. I'm humiliated but can't keep myself from returning to the person who seemed, last night, so glamorous when he showed me around his parents' house.

"Hey Lee," a boy drawls. "What's that fishy smell on you?"

Male laughter. I pretend to ignore what I know is a slur against me.

My father approaches and speaks directly to me, an unusual intervention.

"What d' you think you're doing?" Spoken from his own experience as a young man taking women for his pleasure. "Go help your brother with the boat!"

No garden wedding down a boxwood edged aisle for me, the future Mrs. Kingsman, new bearer of the ancient slave owning name.

17

The Other Black

My college roommate Sarah was my first Jewish friend. We had both come north—she from Bronxville, I from New Jersey—to the University of Vermont. I wanted to get as far away from home as I dared and I did not dare far. I had heard that it was so cold there, girls were allowed to wear pants to class in winter. You could take skiing in gym class. I had visited Vermont once as a small child with my parents and retained images of unbound nature, dirt roads and the luxurious smell of cow manure. I was keen to return.

Sarah's motive was different. Her beloved father had gone to medical school at UVM where he had met Sarah's mother. Sarah was a baby when her father diagnosed his own case of leukemia and died soon thereafter. She wore his phi beta kappa key on her watchband.

Sarah: shy, hardworking, serious. Mimi: naive, hardworking,

eager for excitement. While I blundered into a social life, submitting to blaring fraternity parties and the drunken approaches of dull guys, Sarah stayed in our room working. I thought she was missing something even as social life bored me. I never knew how she felt about dating, if she even wanted to date.

It was from Sarah that I heard about the Rosenbergs, the Soviets, Communism ("It gets things done very fast," she said, in a backward country, by way of Communism's appeal.). I took a World History course, found out about Hitler who had, until that time, only been the source of moronic grade school jokes ("What did Hitler say to his wife after she had a baby? 'Hotsy Totsy, there's another Nazi.'") I learned from Sarah that to be Jewish was to be alert to social harm and suffering in a way to which I was oblivious. The words I had never heard in my parents' house—anti-Semitism, Holocaust, pogrom—were well known facts

So it was a badge of glamour that I was generally thought to be Jewish. My New Jersey voice, my humor, my dark hair and prominent nose. I didn't realize that these were the stereotypes of anti-Semitism. I was proud to be seen as urban, possibly from New York.

I embellished this image with what I thought of as a New York Jewish accent to amuse people while drinking at parties until, at one summer party, in Cape May, someone put a stop to it. "You're being egocentric," he said. I was unfamiliar with the word but I was learning it now and it was something you didn't want to be.

Cal, my future friend, could have said, "Don't be an asshole" or "Shut up"—what a more drunk, less intelligent guy might have said—and it might have been what Cal was thinking but he didn't say it. I appreciated his comment because I wanted to be educated, I wanted to fit in with people like Cal, a young advertising executive who was not fighting in Vietnam because he'd been paralyzed from the waist down by an errant bullet from a hunting rifle.

Be yourself, he seemed to be telling me. Who was that? A white girl from South Jersey. I didn't want to be that.

The next summer in Scotland, where Sarah and I had gone to study, my racism followed me.

"He jewed him down," I said, describing a friend's successful haggling at a used book store for editions of Samuel Johnson's letters.

"I said, 'chewed,'" I pled, when Sarah quietly, seriously, confronted me with the slur.

I was mortified but I could not bring myself to acknowledge what I'd said and Sarah was too wise to continue challenging me. She would leave me to learn for myself.

18

The Underground

The next summer, I am with my parents in Philadelphia. My father is taking my mother and me out to dinner to an Italian restaurant. The choice of restaurant is a rare variation from his preferred prime ribs at a log cabin style restaurant near where we live. Wall murals of indeterminate Italian scenes: cove-side villages, classical ruins. Piped in mandolins. Waiters in dark suits move among the tables, serving plates of spaghetti with a soup spoon for those who require this assistance. A tureen of tomato sauce is brought to the table with a bowl of Parmesan cheese. We eat heartily, happily. My father, who never takes vacations, is now allowing himself Fridays off.

The narrow south Philly streets are clogged with traffic, so we have parked in an underground garage. Outside the restaurant, my mother clasps my arm as we walk toward the garage entrance. My father is slightly ahead of us, keys already in hand. We enter the gloom and follow my father between rows of cars.

A figure approaches. My mother's fingers drill into my elbow. *Jim.* My father cannot hear her. The man wears a light shirt and dark trousers. He is black. *Jim!*

The man is close to us now. My mother begins to run, something I haven't seen her do since I was a child menaced by a neighbor boy.

" *JIM!*" A full-throated, operatic shriek.

My father, at the open door of his car, glances up from lighting a cigarette.

Frantic to get into the car, she pulls me with her into the back seat.

My father glances back. What's the idea?

"*Jim! That man!* "

He turns on the ignition. " *For god sake mother.*"

A car backs out of its parking spot and moves slowly past us. The black driver doesn't look at us.

19

The Other Rosenberg

"Who?" my father narrowed his eyes as if scouting a stranger's face at a distance. I said my boyfriend's name again. The squint turned into a sneer.

By now I knew the dark provenance of that name for men like my father, with rural high school educations who worked with their hands.

I provide a rushed sketch by way of explanation: A boy I met waitressing that summer in Cape May ("I'm your genial host," my gauche, feigned Jewish accent no match for his irony), going to Georgetown, a musician (guitar), poet (songs), just drafted, (Vietnam). From—I name a fancy suburb outside the city.

My father glared at me, silent, dismissive, as I listed Andy Rosenberg's qualities. My father who never taught me how to live, never championed me, never once said 'love,' was now condemning my boyfriend on the associations raised by his name.

He's just stopping to say hello, going to his friend's apartment in New York, advertising executive (the one who had pronounced me egocentric—helpful but as yet unheeded advice).

Perhaps he would absent himself in his workshop while Andy said hello, my father who had never taught me what to do beyond "in life you will have to do things that you don't want to do." The story of the first 40 years of his life. Whose unspoken command was to make him proud, bring home a rich white boy with an expensive car.

Later that day, Andy Rosenberg stands in our living room, glances around with his own ironic sneer. Where to sit. I gesture towards a Victorian love seat. With a roll of his eyes, Andy condemns our house.

My father appears. Andy stands up. My father looks at him wordlessly and squats as if he were outdoors. He will not dignify this meeting by taking a seat. My mother enters the room with a voice stretched tight and high with nerves.

I have no memory of how long Andy stayed but the meeting wasn't so much a meeting as a sighting. My father must have stood up and left the room, rejecting what he had assessed from the position of a farmer or hunter or carpenter, a working man, builder of this country, who had no time to sit.

A year later, after Andy had written me a ponderous letter ("kindness motivates me to tell you") revealing his longtime love, ("Jill and I grew up in California" —place of magic—against which southern New Jersey could not compete), acknowledging the pain his decision to break up would cause me ("there is no equity"), he got back in touch with me.

My father answered the phone next to his bed where he was

preparing for sleep with *The Readers Digest*. I stretched the phone cord into the bathroom and closed the door.

Andy wanted to visit. I enjoyed declining. I was so busy with a summer job and preparing to go to Europe for a year.

"'That viper,'" my father said, as reported to me by my mother the next day.

Jew. Snake. Devil. Was that the direction of his dark associations?

A year later, I met another Rosenberg on a train. He took me to the bar car, gave me his phone number. I met him later at his apartment in Philadelphia for a party. He cleaned a knife smeared with cream cheese by running it down the bridge of my nose. I did not react.

"You're welcome in my life anytime," he said, leaving the choice up to me.

I was fascinated by the boys in the Jewish fraternity at the University of Vermont, boys from expensive suburbs outside New York. UVM was their safety school to which they retreated after being rejected by the Ivies. Swartz, Klein, Mankowitz. Serious about grades and singers of arcane, filthy songs, they were saving themselves for Jewish girls. I did not pass.

Jerome, the solitary Negro at UVM, was also a member of the Jewish fraternity. You shouldn't assume he was a mascot. Jerome would have been happy to be considered Jewish but I doubt he knew about African Jewish sects. He didn't live at the fraternity but would appear at parties and stand snickering in a corner. I once met Jerome in New York's Port Authority station. We had a cup of coffee but I was too inhibited to go outside and walk down the street with him. I claimed I had an appointment.

Cake Walk, or, as it was ominously spelled, Kake Walk, was the high point of fraternity Carnival at UVM, a teeth-clenchingly dull event held on a frigid February weekend and culminating in a glaringly racist event: Walking for the Cake. I don't remember anyone objecting to or even discussing the blackface worn by the pairs of fraternity boys as they locked elbows and high-strutted across a stage in a gross pantomime of a slave holiday ritual. A university Board member in the mid-1960's must have been sufficiently concerned that the blackface was painted greenface to mollify donors. The event was banned altogether the year after I graduated.

20

The Prince

Spring in England during my Junior Year Abroad. I'm wandering through museums while my friend Adele has a Harley Street abortion, a consequence of an encounter in Venice, another story of the 1960s.

England is an extended rainy day, cool and gauzy with new leaves and drifts of daffodils and blue scilla under heritage oaks that have yet to be threatened by the terrifying gales of the future.

My traveling outfit is a tweed skirt, a garter belt and stockings (the Scandinavian girls will be showing up in tights and mini skirts later that summer), and a pink sweater. Something skimpy and impractical on my feet. My hair is pulled back and held by a tortoise shell hair clip I bought on Portobello Road.

I'm drifting around the Tate Gallery in a fog while my friend is at her appointment with death. *Is she on the table? Are they sticking stuff up her? Sucking out blood and a naked baby bird?*

He appears at my side, accompanied by heavy cologne. The blackest of black men. A grey suit tight over muscular shoulders. "Excuse me, Miss." A velvet murmur ending in a prolonged sibilance.

I look into this unknown face. He must be African. Africa is a continent but it might as well be one big country for all I know.

"*I think you might be a princess.*" Prin cess. That elete hiss again.

Even I am not too naïve to recognize this come-on. His head slightly tilted, his hair shaved close, black moss.

I have been taught to answer every question. No, I'm an American.

Ah! His wide smile reveals a trove of gold.

Unguarded as a child, I question the three parallel scars that decorate each of his cheeks. Tiny spears.

My fathah. Ees a king. The carefully enunciated syllables of colonial English.

I stare at the incisions. Was he forbidden to scream when the knife cut him? The edges of the slits have widened around a smooth matte interior.

Fifty years later, I will see a statuesque African American museum guard in gold earrings and intricate braids piled in an elaborate headdress. I gaze up at his beauty. My old age has opened the door to a cache of love which I enjoy bestowing.

"If you don't mind my saying—"

He looks down at me.

"You are a work of art yourself."

Startled, he laughs. "Well thank you," he says softly. "I appreciate that."

I am flooded with happiness.

But I am still decades away from this scene. I ask the prince why he is in London.

I am studying banking. The carefully enunciated consonants of his colonial British accent. *And you? Are you on a world tour?*

He skillfully guides me with the lightest touch to my elbow, as one might direct a well-trained equine. On the steps of the museum he offers me the scene with the palm of one hand.

"London agrees with me very much," he announces. "Let me show you." Here is the dry cleaner where he takes his suits, the green grocer, the tobacconist. Do I smoke? His mother says that women who smoke are witches. A flash of white as he rolls his eyes, utters a brief high laugh, an African sound that is new to me.

Do I live in a city? No? He will not ever live anywhere else. Cities suit him.

A line of shabby greystones in Bayswater. "Please." He allows me to proceed him into a dusty vestibule and up dim stairs to the second floor, unlocks a door on more of that cloying scent.

The room is dingy, neat. A single bed, bureau and chair. A desk with papers, books, pens neatly ordered. Please, sit down. He pulls out his desk chair, arranges it facing the room. *They're packing Adele's vagina, giving her big sanitary pads to take back to her hotel where she is staying with her mother. Her mother! Who has flown to be with her and is in the waiting room.*

He pours a glass of thick red liqueur and holds it out to me.

I accept it, sleepwalking in full daylight. The sugary taste is cloying like his cologne.

Now he's opening the lid of a portable record player, removing a disc from its cover, holding it with the tips of his surprisingly long fingers. He is sweating through the underarms of his suit.

Something I have never heard like a deeper, more frantic calypso. (My uncle likes Harry Bellafonte. Calypso is a fad among their friends who go to a club somewhere in southern New Jersey. *I had to leave a little girl in Kingston Town.* Harry Belafonte's smooth, caramel face on the cover. A reassuring face that suggests white ancestry. *Creole ladies with flashing eyes.*)

In truth, I don't remember the music, just his elegant matte black fingers as he adjusted the disk on the little turntable and lowered the tone arm. Then he turned to me.

Why was I here? Why did I drink the candied liquid? That we were in dance position was only a pretense. This was prelude to the seduction he practiced in his room with any girl who would accept his invitation.

But I hadn't accepted. I hadn't done anything. I had no known motives while my friend had her abortion. I felt nothing. I was sleep walking into a scene like the one that resulted in Adele's ordeal, at that moment, on Harley Street.

He tightened his clasp on my back and ground his pelvis against me.

I pulled away; I had to be with my friend who needed an abortion.

Oh, this is not a problem, he held his fingers up, splayed, ten solutions. My sistah is a nurse, she can find the best place for your friend, best doctor.

No. I must go. I broke through my passivity like a storybook princess from her spell. As I fled, the sound of his protests followed me down the staircase to the street.

If he were white, would I have taken off my clothes and let him toy with me?

I was still unfamiliar with birth control, there being little access to it yet. The pill was only for rich girls, sophisticates or possibly the daughters of kings, whose fathers could pay. Girls who knew how to take care of themselves.

21

Afro

The summer before my senior year, I'm up to nothing, bored, with a car. I'm wandering, snooping around after Cal, friend of the Rosenberg boy who explained the inequity of love and who is now in Vietnam.

Eleven AM and I'm knocking on the door of a Philly apartment where Cal is staying. Why am I doing this? No idea. The door is opened by a light-skinned black girl with an Afro. Creole ladies with flashing eyes. Claudine. I'm with Billy. She mentions Cal's friend. The apartment is stuffed with people behind closed doors, sleeping off a big party. Lots of dope and acid. Cal is still asleep. *He was on a big trip.* No, she doesn't think he'll be waking up anytime soon.

I've never taken acid. Afraid if I did, I'd never be the same. Same? Which is how? A college girl who has applied to graduate school.

I follow her into the living room. Two couches, a stereo, a straight back chair and a bay window. Claudine wears shorts, a tank top and sandals. She has long delicate legs and arms, a long neck. She sits very straight on the straight back chair, crosses her legs, picks up a glass of water from the windowsill, sips, replaces the glass. This gesture will be repeated through my visit. Lift, sip, replace. The glass seems never to empty. She picks up what looks like a tuning fork from the windowsill and begins poking through her enormous halo of hair.

How do I know Cal? She asks mildly, as something to say. Where do I live? She nods, understanding about New Jersey. Do I like it there?

She and Billy want to get an apartment in a more interesting part of Philly I've never heard of. Billy plays there and she backs him up on vocals. *Vocals.* Lots of hippies in that part of town.

Hippies. A new word to me. I stare at her. I imagine kids jiggling their hips. *You know,* she explains, *hippies have discovered a new way of living.* She smiles. I understand, right?

I grew my hair long like Joan Baez. When I saw Bob Dylan I was wearing a madras dress and black tights to hide my thighs.

Hippies, she says, are new. Part of a revolution. She uncrosses those graceful bare legs, grooms her hair with the prong.

Do I want a glass of water?

No thanks, I'd better go. Tell Cal 'hi' for me.

What's your name again?"

I realize I never told her.

22

Electric Carving Knife

It's still the Vietnam time. My parents have retired to rural New England and I am making one last visit to New Jersey en route to graduate school in Chicago.

I'm staying with my childhood friend who had the black roommate. Connie is now married and her husband is in Danang and she is living with her parents. Connie hangs out the flag every morning in honor of our military.

I haven't given the war much thought since I decided to go to graduate school. I've been told the University of Chicago is an elite school. I am proud to have been accepted but uneasy that I don't have the talent to do well.

The suspicion that I am not beautiful or talented has dogged me throughout childhood and never more than when someone from South Jersey compliments me. A self-hating snob, I believe that no one here has real brilliance. Unless you're a Quaker you must fight your way out.

Connie's house is much as I remember it when we were twelve and her mother told us to stay away from *creole ladies with flashing eyes* which I now, as an English major and an interpreter of all things, assume means the allure of Negro culture.

I've just arrived and have been taken upstairs by Connie's mom to drop off my suitcase on a twin bed in Connie's childhood bedroom, pink with candy striped café curtains.

Dinner is roast meat with pasty gravy, boiled potatoes and peas. Everyone has a glass of white wine, a sophisticated upgrade Connie has made to family dinners since her marriage.

Connie's dad says a one sentence grace and we toast our loved ones in the military. He begins slicing the roast with an electric carving knife. A tiny whir accompanies the separation and slow descent of each piece of meat. I stare out the picture window into the back yard, an unadorned square of lawn. Connie's mom sees me looking.

"I don't have your mother's green thumb," she explains. My mother is held up as a domestic benchmark: homemade bread, homemade jam, pachysandra and forsythia.

I consider my family more sophisticated than Connie's. My mother was trained as an artist and my father is a builder, a highly ingenious man. As a child, Connie told me her father was too smart to go in the army while my father endured 4 years in the Middle East. These comparisons stay with me since I recognized them in elementary school. But later I realized that Connie's mother may have been reassuring her about her father's patriotic war work in the face of the nastiness and ignorance of her little classmates.

I accept a plate and pass the gravy boat. No one has anything to say. I sense that I, the guest, am meant to provide conversation. Or is it the mention of my mother, now wrenched from her childhood home to follow my father into retirement in the boonies of Maine, that conjures up my father's long ago slur in the Ladies' restaurant and causes me to open my mouth?

"My dad heard this joke." I have the table's attention. Grins of anticipation.

"What's the headline when a colored astronaut goes into space?"

They don't know. Eager, smiling, waiting for the punch.

"Coon on the moon."

Connie's mom lets out a tiny squeal, claps.

"I'm not finished! There's another headline: 'The Jig is Up.'"

Connie's dad chuckles his approval.

This might be a good time to stop but I remember a third and more risqué joke.

"Two colored fashion models are having pictures taken. The photographer gets them in position and goes behind his camera."

'What he gonna do now?' says one girl.

'He gonna focus,' says the other girl.

'Bofus?'"

Connie's mother purses her lips, cuts her eye at me. *Oh, that Mimi.*

If I feel superior to these people, why did I need to tell those jokes? To fit in? To be a star in their world?

I loved Connie and I still do. We were allies through puberty and teens and have remained close friends in spite of our differences. After she left college and wanted to marry her boyfriend—a desire her mother resisted by putting Connie under virtual house arrest during the summer—my father paid for her bus fare and gave me his car keys to drive her to the bus station in Philadelphia. We never admitted our secret role in the elopement and we always felt justified.

After dinner, Connie and I go to bed early. Deep in the night, I have one of my screaming nightmares. I wake up sweating.

Backstory. I was nearly raped in Venice—a scene not unlike the one with the prince in London. Meanwhile, my travelling companion Adele allowed her attacker to rape her and got pregnant and I almost immediately began having screaming nightmares—a faceless struggle threatens my life and ends with me shrieking in a churning vortex of terror.

That I should have such a dream in my childhood friend's bedroom floods me with humiliation. I must have been attacked by my own guilt at telling those jokes.

These dreams are vengeful furies. But I seem to have waked no one, not even Connie in the other twin bed. The next morning no one says anything.

23

Blackstone Rangers

Four days after the screaming nightmare, I've moved into a graduate dorm on the South Side of Chicago because it's said to be safer than an apartment. Be careful, people have told me, don't leave the campus. The University is surrounded by slums. I hear shots in the night.

This is a busy time for me, adjusting to the university, buying books, organizing a class schedule. I feel like I'm living in a gothic cloister. I'd be happy if we wore academic gowns like the undergraduates I saw at Oxford during my year abroad. I wish I was elite enough to attain the full court academic fantasy—but this is as close to the ivory tower as I will get.

Slowly I realize that events are unfolding in Chicago, chaotic, threatening to others but I can't connect, feel nothing. The National Guard has just left the playing fields across from my dorm. I see the last military trucks and jeeps driving away. They were here to quell riots after Martin Luther King was shot. First King, then Bob Kennedy. A busy time for the police.

The morning after my arrival at the dorm, I walk outside to another scene I can't place or fathom, a meeting of two rival gangs on the field where the National Guard has just decamped. The South Side Disciples and the Black Stone Rangers are going to make a truce. Stay away. Stay inside. I watch from a gothic window as a phalanx of black men in sunglasses and tight white t-shirts over muscled chests arrange themselves as a barrier separating gang members from idling police cars ringing the field, lights flashing. Two opposing gang leaders approach each other, slowly, and stop at the center of the field. I watch with the others graduate students, mostly foreign—Indians, Asians, some Europeans. Nothing happens. I become bored and go back to studying.

The summer of 1968 will be considered historic. Vietnam is raging, Eugene McCarthy is running for President. Those hippies I heard about from the young black girl in Philadelphia as she preened her hair are now a force requiring Mayor Daley to crack down at the Democratic National Convention. Mayor Daley, my father says, is the right mayor for this time. I know he means that the mayor would beat on the Black Panthers and hippies. I don't know anything about these groups although I've seen photos of Fred Hampton and Abbie Hoffman. I'm annoyed by my father's get-tough attitude but I don't want to be involved.

My detachment isn't too different from my brother Jim's. He's in Chicago, too, in his first year of law school on the North Side of the city. He got a deferment for an ailment that today would be called IBS. He's renting an apartment with Micky, a smart guy and, like Jim, a standard issue misogynist, by which I mean he and Jim treat women as objects. They both sleep with "stews" as they call stewardesses. Jim, the more romantic of the two, hums "Leaving on a Jet Plane." Their lives depress me and now, as I write this, I am not surprised that Micky lived with his mother until her death and has inherited her house. Jim, on the other hand, married a lovely woman whom he treats with a mixture of respect and fear. But I'm writing about 1969 when conventional women, such as myself, felt incomplete if they weren't identified with a man. We knew we weren't fulfilled by most relationships but we didn't know why.

That summer I roomed next door to Lois and Madeleine, two Sacred Heart nuns in civilian clothes who are getting their PhDs, and a black girl named Bethany with old fashioned processed hair and skirts to her knees. I acquired a boyfriend from suburban Chicago with a low draft number. We're all English majors. The nuns, Bethany and I, sometimes study in a university reading room. One afternoon, as we leave an exam, Lois mutters, "That test worked me like a nigger."

Bethany's face does not change. No one says anything. We agree, the test was a real bitch.

My boyfriend Chet and I sleep together on weekends. I might have had my first orgasm with him, I'm not sure. When I want to try again to confirm what I felt, he refuses. "Don't demand it," he says. Although we keep sleeping together, I do not experience another orgasm. That's a sad detail but I want to include it for psycho-sexual context.

I had never felt such heat as summer in Chicago. Thunderstorms went on all night and the lightning flashed purple. One particularly hot weekend, my boyfriend and I went to the beach to swim. We unfurled our towels among black couples with boom boxes. *It's your thing. Do what you want to do.* Driving back to the dorm, I saw a bumper sticker: *BLACK IS BEAUTIFUL*. "No it's not." I was shocked to hear my mental reply. The bumper sticker felt like an assault on the inherited image of black people as outside the white standard of beauty.

Later that summer, in my dorm room, I wake from another nightmare. I am silent at breakfast as two girls mention hearing a woman scream during the night.

I'd never thought of myself as a woman. The second wave of feminism hadn't hit yet.

"Scary. Sounded like she was being attacked."

It would be good to identify my psychic assailant here in this protected academic environment. College and graduate school were places to hide. The idea was: don't learn anything; stay in your brain cage; obey the orders of some academic don. The screaming nightmare was me being assaulted by memory, trying to escape the cage.

24

Cigar Ash

Sure, I signed the loyalty oath saying I wouldn't protest on campus, wouldn't occupy academic buildings. I'd also developed what I thought of as the "Mr. Jones theory of modern life." As the lyrics to the Dylan song went: *you know something is happening here but you don't know what it is.* My friends laughed but I was serious. I knew the world was being powerfully disrupted; I didn't know how or why. But at least I knew that I didn't know.

That summer, I was told that to finish my degree I needed another foreign language. Spanish was supplied and I was enrolled in a night course at an adult night school held in an old high school building on the South Side.

We were a class of about 20. Eighteen working class black people coming from their day jobs, a conscientious Bangladeshi man in a suit and tie, and me in a miniskirt and Mary Quant headband. Our grandmotherly teacher, herself probably coming from a day spent teaching high school Spanish, translated 'amigo' as 'old chap.' She wanted everyone to pass.

On the last day of class, three black girls near me turned around in their chairs and asked me what I was doing there. I didn't mention the university when I told them I needed the course to graduate. "That's why I'm here, too," said a young woman. We smiled. I felt that perhaps I had a comrade.

The thing to do on a summer weekend in Chicago was to find an authentic black bar. How did you know it was authentic? Hugo, who was writing his economics dissertation with Milton Friedman, claimed to be an expert in seeking the most obscure places. As part of his extracurricular education, Hugo was in the midst of an affair with a young black woman. He said he was still shocked by the feel of her hair.

"*'Ah wanna know what Hugo think bout dat,'*" he quoted the girl's mother at her breakfast table and laughed with mock self-effacement that these people should value crumbs from his intellect.

Hugo's dalliance provided him what he considered a deeper understanding of black social norms. He reminded us that we needed to dress nicely to go to this bar. Show some respect. No hippie outfits. These were authentic black people. So I put on a pink linen mini dress my mother had made me, pantyhose and heels. That evening, Hugo and his housemate Sheila (PhD candidate, linguistics, wearing a Nantucket sundress) Chet, of the rationed orgasms, and I drove to someplace in the dark.

I'd never been in an all-black bar, an all-black anything. The Tik Tok Lounge was on a quiet street outside the jazz district with several open parking spaces, indicating that we were far from the popular white entertainment zone. A flat black vestibule with no bouncer and the nose stopping scent of coconut air freshener opened into a small club, also flat black. The place was about half full. Middleaged couples sat at tables around a sparsely populated dance floor. The bandstand was empty. A song I didn't recognize ended and couples made their way to their tables. Hugo said the house band was off. We found a vacant table and ordered.

Chet and Hugo discussed this neighborhood neither really knew but had opinions about, while I grew increasingly bored. I watched other tables, my attention taken by a May/December couple slowly exiting the dance floor. A woman in an auburn wig and a blue satin dress was being led carefully to her table by her partner, a much younger man with slicked back hair like Chuck Berry. It occurred to me that she might be his mother and this bar was a beloved haven for the neighborhood.

The music started, rose in velocity and suddenly people were crowding onto the dance floor. Should we join them? A man stopped at my chair, held out the pink palm of one hand. Dance?

I looked at my friends. No one said anything so I got up and let the man guide me. A familiar somnambulist feeling settled, a caul of unknowing.

The man wore a shiny grey suit over muscular shoulders. We were the same height. He held me closer than the African prince in London. I felt hips, cock, heat. He was crushing my freshly ironed pink dress but I didn't know how to stop him, a twenty-two-year-old woman with no volition.

It occurred to me that this display was part of bar culture, it was what people came to see, perhaps what Chet and Hugo wanted to see.

When the music stopped, the man returned me to my table and disappeared. Nobody said anything. Chet went to the bar for more beers. Hugo was leaning back in his chair smoking a cigar to great effect. I'd never seen him smoke but perhaps a cigar accompanied the rich experience of slumming. He took a long drag, exhaled and carefully tipped cigar ash on my knee, burning a wide run up my pantyhose.

25

Midwest

I moved to Peoria because the college there offered me a job. Kids were dropping out and cashing in their savings bonds to join communes but my major concern had been drilled into me since childhood: *you must be able to support yourself*, a weak substitute for my parents' true desire: *a man to support you.*

The head of the hiring committee took me out for lunch to a Chinese restaurant. I had nothing to say while I forked down chow mein. I knew nothing about the town, so this kindly academic gave me an overview of neighborhoods where I might want to rent an apartment. Downtown was putting up its first condos. Since I was coming from Chicago I might like that. Outside of town were ranch developments if I wanted to rent an entire house with more space, although most faculty preferred to live nearer campus. Many homeowners rented out entire floors in their lovely old Victorians on a bluff overlooking the Illinois

River. And then there was low cost housing near the industrial area on the river, home to the black population. "It's an unusual location," he acknowledged. " But some faculty members have chosen to live there."

Who was this guy trying to kid? Was he seriously presenting this "location" as a likely choice for a single 23- year-old white girl, or was he just covering all his liberal bases?

Not that liberalism was in the ascendancy. As a single woman and the youngest faculty member, I was preyed on by the dean of students (grabbed my ass and squeezed, hard, at an opening reception) and a male committee chair (asked me for a ride home from a meeting and lunged for my crotch as I pulled up in front of his house), but I was excluded from all faculty parties. Young, single, potential competition for a faculty wife.

One fall afternoon, the football team pursued my car around town, horns beeping. The next morning, I found their gift on my front seat: a package of condoms pierced with needles and a note: *To the perfect teacher from her oh so grateful students.*

There was no recourse. The term "sexual harassment" was unknown. I piled furniture against my third floor apartment door at night after someone mounted a 3 hour buzzer fest down in the vestibule.

The semester passed. Abbie Hoffmann showed up to abuse the student audience and scratch his crotch while his barefoot paramour leapt about the stage like a witch's familiar. I never would have believed that several decades later, the father of my child would write Hoffman's biography, among several other books.

The young white guy who taught the new Black Studies

course at the college taped a slogan to his office door: *If you're not part of the solution, you're part of the problem.* I didn't know what the solution was so I assumed I must be part of the problem. I yearned to return to the University of Chicago where a problem in a Shakespeare quarto kept me busy one entire weekend puzzling out which word the bard intended when Hamlet uttered, "oh that this too too *sullied/ sallied/ or solid* flesh should melt... ."

Despite trying to convince my American literature class that Joel Chandler Harris was black (a student corrected me), I was offered a second year contract. Near the end of term, the Shakespeare teacher and the gym teacher, a lesbian couple, invited me to dinner and gave me a directive: *get out while you can.*

That I did. The so-called sexual revolution was speeding up. The teacher who grabbed my crotch on the way home from a party was now begging me to sublet him my apartment as his hideaway for his affair with the lesbian Shakespearean. My phone fights with Chet were so loud that the people downstairs began pounding on the ceiling with a broom. Woodstock passed me by. The black power movement was beginning to irritate some of the more conservative faculty. My closet lesbian office mate who could have passed for an old maid began a habit of crooning "BLAAAAAACK PEOPLEEEEE" when she caught sigh of African American students walking outside or sitting on the desiccated grass of the quadrangle. I ignored her but I would have been better off switching offices.

26

Montreal

After picking up my MA certificate, I left for Montreal where I knew no one but had been offered a teaching fellowship. *Friendly, familiar, foreign and near.* Initially Canada felt like none of those things. I spoke infantile New Jersey French and the province was in the middle of a separatist crisis. I had no idea what was going on. McGill was a cold Anglo institution beset by student rioters. I mailed invitations to students and neighbors in my condo, gave parties in my tiny studio apartment and haphazardly made a few friends.

One snowy night Harry, an economist from down the hall, and I were sitting on the electric radiator smoking dope and looking down at the car rodeo that preceded the city's snow removal. Two black men rounded the corner pushing an old Dodge Dart. Bearing down on them from behind was the parking tow truck, lights flashing, horn sounding.

"I'll be right back," Harry put on his boots and coat.

I blanched. "Do you think it's safe?"

His expression sagged. *Of course it's safe. These guys need help.*

I sat high up in my warm perch watching Harry supply the extra muscle to move the disabled car to safety. One of the black men reached into his pocket and I had to repress Chicago reactions. No, Harry gestured, palms outward. He didn't want to be paid. The three men shook hands and went their ways.

The next year, I married one of my students as a way of placating my mother who demanded that I not share a bed with a man before marriage. She also wanted the fun of "marrying you out of our own house," as she put it.

"But how will he support you?" she asked, ever faithful to her dream.

Julian Levitt was four years younger than I, unemployed, supported by his father.

"What kind of name," my father demanded, after meeting him. "With that black beard like a Russian." He said "*Russian*" as if he meant "Rasputin," evil. "Must be Jewish."

I told him that Julian said Levitt was Huguenot and that his ancestors migrated from Holland to England and then to Canada. My father didn't buy it.

The wedding was held at my parents' house and my mother made my dress. A dispensation was granted from a Catholic diocese in Montreal and my mother's Catholic priest was procured. My friend Adele drove up from New York to be my maid of honor.

The day before the wedding, my mother and I were primping the geraniums in the first floor window boxes when we noticed a car parked down the road, at a curve. I recognized Julian's father's Land Rover. His father's bald head was visible above the roof—he must have been standing on the running board—with binoculars propped for balance, getting a bead on our house. A woman's head appeared—Julian's stepmother—and he passed her the binoculars.

"Sweet Jesus," my mother said. "That's the family you're marrying into?" Probably one of her own mother's expressions. I doubted if this marriage would live up to her expectations.

The ceremony, hurriedly written by Julian and me, was held in my parents' living room. Unbeknownst to us, the priest added "love, honor, and serve." There was nothing I could do after the words were spoken, so I inexplicably kissed this clergyman.

At the small dinner held in my parents' dining room, Julian's father and stepmother stood at furthest remove from Julian's dithery blond mother whom neither had seen since their marriage fifteen years previous. Julian and I left after dinner to return to student life in Montreal.

An undergraduate with nocturnal habits, Julian rarely saw me. Occasionally we met in bed. I recall disagreements. During one argument, Julian kicked in a kitchen cupboard. During another, he tossed an antique bedside table, part of my trousseau, lovingly refinished by my father, out the window of our flat, down two stories into the front garden where I'd just planted petunias. I slept in a sleeping bag that night, cleaned up the broken glass the next morning and ordered a new window. This incident did not warrant sharing during my feminist consciousness raising meeting that week. Julian and I divorced three years later.

I'd done my duty to my mother and sustained the unfathomable contradictions of middle class propriety.

Radical feminism and bisexual promiscuity rushed in to fill the gap left by my brief monogamy. The polyglot, multiracial, multi-cultural streets of Montreal and the whimsical benevolence of Quebec, even during the separatist crisis, was a revelation. Parties went on all night. During one spectacular blizzard that closed down main roads, I skied down town to a romantic assignation.

One winter night I was hunkered down with my friend Patrick, an American draft resister, and his girlfriend Annie smoking dope. Patrick's girlfriend, a Chinese Canadian, had just picked up a roll of developed photos she'd taken at her family reunion in Toronto. As the dope began to make everything hilarious, Annie spread out her new photos.

"Look!" she pointed, gasping with laughter. "Look how tiny my aunt is. And those twins!" she pointed at two toddlers. "Oh my god!" She swayed back and forth, laughing. "My crazy family. Look at my mom!" She pointed at a woman. I couldn't see the difference between these people. All Chinese. All the same. I let the marijuana take the edge off my boredom as Patrick and Annie laughed about the photographs.

The economy was booming in Montreal and it was easy to get teaching jobs at the new city schools that educated each wave of immigrants seeking shelter from their violent, war-torn homelands. Beautiful young people of all races and classes seemed to me, at least superficially, to be making their way with surprising ease in their new home, scandalizing their more conservative parents by choosing partners from other cultures and races.

But not everyone was comfortable, especially those still struggling to learn the nuances of English. Anthony (Li Sung) sat in the front row of my composition class, head bent over his notebook, trying to copy every word I spoke, then asking me to correct his dictation.

One winter morning, I arrived in class with the beginning of a head cold. Anthony was at his perch. Before I began speaking, I suggested that he push his desk back a few feet because "I'm afraid I might spit on you." Anthony stared at me, his expression hardening, eyes narrowed. He pushed his desk back as I'd asked him to do. After class, he took his notebook and rushed from the room without asking me to review his work. Perhaps he wasn't feeling well. The next class he was silent, did not make eye contact with me, did his work and left.

When it came time for me to return the midterm essays, Anthony took his paper without comment and left. I followed him out.

"Something's wrong," I touched his arm and he jerked it away. "Please tell me how I can help."

"Help?" he let out a yip of derision. "You say you will spit on me. That is what you say. That is how you..." he found the word "...treat me." His eyes blazed at me.

Oh no no no. I apologized, explained. I'd had a cold. I didn't want him to inhale droplets of my spit.

He looked at me hesitantly. I apologized again. *Please believe me. I would never think such a thing. I respect you.*

But I still didn't know what I believed or how I fit in a city whose culture I was too lazy to fully understand or embrace.

Even later, when I was writing freelance, I would be known as *the American*.

The proudly parochial nature of Quebec nationalism bred its own casual racism against black immigrants.

"You know we cannot assume they fully understand or care about our living standards," said an officious Quebecois at a community rental board meeting. I was secretly, cravenly gratified. White Americans weren't the only racists.

But more glaring than racism against blacks in Canada is the bigotry and abuse of Canada's large Indigenous population. My personal experience with native people is limited to students—all positive—in the classroom and a few social interactions in the homes of native activists, two recent events show the hostility, amounting to systemic racism and, in the latter case, terrorism. A young Native woman dying in a Joliette, Quebec hospital was verbally insulted and abused by nurses as she begged for help. She had the presence of mind to film the abuse on her cell phone. This document was shown to the press, police, and native elders after her death. Also, long-standing conflict between Aboriginal and commercial Nova Scotia lobster fishers resulted in recent arson and the destruction of the Mic Mac tribe's moderate livelihood lobster facility. The facility had enabled natives to provide their tribal group with subsistence fishing out of season, when legally necessary. Long simmering resentments among fishers (the Nova Scotia story) and racist attitudes towards Native people generally (the Joliette story) persist all over Canada.

My Cousin Rankin, the son of my father's sister, Aunt Lou, was the one member of my family I know who evolved beyond racism but I still do not know how. A brilliant student ten years older than I, Rankin got a full scholarship to Princeton, went to Union Theological Seminary and became a Presbyterian minister. He gave up the offer of a lucrative Scarsdale parish in order to go south with the Freedom Riders. Rankin worked in Harlem with an African American ministry and, sometime in the early 70s, moved with his wife and young family to California to set up Caesar Chavez's migrant ministry.

"Rankin's a crusader," was my mother's comment on her nephew.

Yes, Rankin was a Christian. But a Crusader? A soldier for Christ? Rankin spent his life working for social justice. As Republicans, my family's sense of justice stopped at the individual level.

When the grape boycott went national and then international, I began joining UFW demonstrations in Montreal. We held picket lines outside food stores in all seasons, even the frigid depths of winter. I was amazed when Rankin came to Montreal to speak in a church basement. He was glad to see me but I was relieved that he was too busy to do more than briefly chat. I felt illegitimate. I didn't know any Latinos but I supported farm workers because Rankin had brought their issues to our family's attention. Rankin was the family celebrity, in my opinion, although I never heard anyone talk about him beyond my mother's "crusader" comment. My brother did not mention Rankin or his activities.

This was still the 1970s when beautiful young white Quebeçoises had seraphic mixed race babies with black men they met at bars or at the drum fests in the park. I would admire these women with their long legs, long dreads, riding their bikes with their beautiful offspring in baby seats.

One morning when I was working in my front garden, a neighbor, Linda stopped to chat and, over that summer we became good friends. Linda was obsessed with black men and slept with many. She claimed not to be attracted to the sex but the racial celebrity which held her in awe of anyone with dark skin, from a disaffected Haitian college professor, to a striving Senegalese presser at a high-end dry cleaner. "He does all the wedding dresses," Linda told me. And, indeed, Nabby's long, delicate fingers seemed the perfect instruments for smoothing the individual satin folds of a shirred waist.

I participated in Linda's adoration of the impeccable table manners of her men who dropped not one grain of rice ("because they waste nothing") in comparison to Canadian diners.

She learned bits of their tribal languages, wired money home to their families, but she did not want a commitment of middle class proportions. Linda discussed these men, speculated about them, quoted them constantly but she did not want to bring a black man home as her partner.

I was confused by the motives behind Linda and other young white women's fascination with black men. Did her attachment to these men go deeper than the color of their skin? I accompanied Linda to African music clubs but I would not pretend to be comfortable outside my own tribe. I joined a Congolese dance class that I loved and attended for years but I didn't get to know the drummers who transported our bodies and spirits or the beautiful teacher from Congo-Brazzaville. Something in my attitude to black people was occluded.

One summer afternoon, I bumped into my old schoolmate Sammy Boyd. Newly divorced and with a teenaged son, Sammy, now Samuel, lived not far from me. I invited him to dinner along with my friend Tony to witness this radical scene: I was making dinner for a black friend.

I made stir fried shrimp and Samuel showed me a wallet photo he carried of his son, Amin, a hefty light skinned boy with an afro. We talked about mutual friends from long ago, our divorces, our work. Our common identities as Americans in French Canada overcame our racial differences. Over my years in Montreal, I would run into Samuel but it wasn't until much later that the Internet reconnected us.

In the mid-'70s, an American friend took me to visit Total Loss Farm, a southern Vermont commune. It was paradise, a rural world like what my father described in his stories of farm life. I milked the cow and shot a stream of warm milk directly from the teat into a barn cat's mouth. It was here that I met and began seeing Gabriel Ross, an anti-war no nukes activist and a writer. I was surprised that he could accept someone with no activist affiliation beyond the vaguest freestyle feminism. Gabriel's friends had gone to jail for their beliefs. I signed the University of Chicago loyalty oath: do not disrupt institutional life.

Although, in the eyes of my family, I was a hairy-legged, hairy-armpitted outlier, my parents seemed to accept Gabriel, yet another Jew. My father was polite, until I came to him for a loan to buy an apartment in Montreal.

"Here you are, a girl 30 years old and you're still without a man to provide for you. All I wanted was to see you pull into our driveway with. ...." I know, Dad. I was weeping by the time he grudgingly dispensed the loan.

But my father needn't have despaired. My drive to provide for my own financial security still overshadowed my ability to love. That is, until Gabriel and I had our daughter. By the time Kathryn was born, our relationship was unraveling. Kathryn held us together for a decade before we separated. We always put our daughter's needs first and, ultimately, we became friends and our family reunited around our new partners and stepchildren. I'm making it seem too easy. Separating from my daughter and then reuniting and healing have been the most difficult acts of my adult life and the ones of which I am most proud.

I would not have been able to navigate this primary loss and reconciliation without the attendant eight years of Jungian analysis. I do not want to unpack the details of this work beyond mentioning a connection to racism that remains, for me, unresolved.

As typically happens to people undergoing analysis, my dreams became vivid, full of Jungian imagery. Black people. Native Americans. Asians. Indians. They all began showing up in my dreams. Jungians identify these figures as manifestations of my shadow, carrying weaknesses, insecurities. According to Jungians, the shadow is universally dark. To me, the shadow's properties had to be socially, culturally conditioned. The shadow is endemic and eternal but so is racism.

27

Vermont

After nearly a decade alone, teaching in Montreal and doing Jungian work, I was introduced to my future husband Rick, at a Vermont barbecue. I was sorry that my father did not live to meet Rick but at least my mother was there to absorb the full effect of his beauty and his deep WASP pedigree stretching back to Puritanism. When Rick's mother's family gathers together to ask the Lord's blessing each Thanksgiving, they are summoning their pilgrim ancestors in a big way.

Rick's father's family emigrated from Sweden in the 19th century. His earliest ancestor is black. Rick's great-great-great grandfather, a North African, was enslaved to the 18th century French court of Marie Antoinette and later taken to Sweden as a kettledrummer to the king. His contemporary Swedish descendants are proud of their ancestor and hold a biannual family reunion, during which they commemorate him. Some of the older relatives show off details of their own facial structure and hair that resemble their black forebear.

Rick told me that his own father and grandfather never mentioned their black relative. "When it came down to it," Rick said, "They were racists." Rick likes to tell the story of his African ancestor but I am not sure where he stands on systemic racism, because I have been reticent to ask and I don't want to know. In this way, I would be reflecting my mother's attitudes.

About a decade ago, Rick and I accompanied a group of the American relatives traveling to Stockholm for one of these family reunions. The Swedes treated us with lavish hospitality and took us, as the interpretive plaques said, *in the footsteps of our ancestors*, some of whose steps had been cast in bronze in the city's cobblestone squares. A Danish film crew followed us for the week of our visit, as part of their film project about Scandinavians in search of their African roots. Of the more than one hundred family members they could have filmed, the crew stuck closest to Rick, the blondest, most Nordic and least African of the group.

"Photogenic," said one of Rick's sisters, when I speculated on why the film crew didn't focus on different subjects.

Vermont, where we live now, is the second whitest state in the nation. I have no black friends here although I know the names of the black activists in our state and I recognize black people who live in our town, (there are few).

When I taught high school English for the Vermont Department of Corrections, only one of my male students was black, a beautiful tall boy with several children living elsewhere. I helped him write letters to his girlfriend. I don't know what he thought of this old lady sitting across a picnic table from him. I didn't know how to help him. Decades later, I still see him, walking with a child for an ice cream cone, smoking with friends. He's not in jail but I don't know if he has a job. I wave to him from my car but he doesn't recognize me.

My English classes at a state college in New Hampshire were divided by class, not race. Many of my students were the first in their family to attend college. Their toehold at the school was tenuous. Any economic disruption at home—a parent's illness, job loss, divorce—could result in their needing to quit school.

"That's a knock-off Fendi," a girl muttered to her friend about another girl's purse.

"Yeah," the owner said. "I got it on a trip to China." Touché. Class status was the smack down. Although the state shares a border with Canada, most of my students had never left the eastern U.S.

The few assiduously recruited African American students were not reticent to point out unacknowledged racism in the classroom and racial profiling in the community. Most young men said they had been stopped by the police while driving, for no offense.

In our town, I always smile at black people on the street, to make eye contact even as I wonder if I'm patronizing.

Before the Covid shutdown, I was sitting in a Department of Children and Families team meeting for an African American woman and her children. I am a Guardian ad Litem, a family court-appointed advocate for children who, through no fault of their own, are in state custody. I was one of three white people in a room of six African American and Latina social workers, day care providers and other supports for this young mother. The case was overdue for closure—either family reunification or adoption—yet ambiguity continued. I took notes as each person provided an update on her work with the children and mother. The kids were thriving in foster care and the mother's situation was murky. There was an issue of potential fraud, of paramours exhibiting unsafe behaviors. The mother defended herself calmly and repeatedly questioned why the others were not acting in good faith because she was.

I am proud of the children's resilience. How could I deny them reunion with their mother and siblings? Would they be safe? Did we have hard evidence to bring against the mother? Or were we falling back on stereotype? I watched her relatives, patient women who had taken time off work to come to this meeting and were as concerned as I was that this woman's life be put right. They were prepared to help. She had a support system but, of course, the decision was up to the state. They were not trying to upend a system that, at best, was imperfect. Yes, their young relative was headstrong and had made mistakes but she was maturing. "Just a late starter," said her aunt, and the young mother laughed, rolled her eyes.

28

Twin

My brother's struggle is part of my own struggle and part of this writing. We shared the same racial attitudes until I moved further away from home—Chicago, Montreal, Vermont—and began feeling differently.

Jim and I look nothing alike. Once blond and slim, now white haired and brawny, Jim looks the part of a successful businessman while I'm petite and casual with dyed brown closely cropped hair. I cling to the hope that I look much younger than my 74 years. People are shocked to discover we are twins.

Jim stayed close to home and, even now, lives five miles from where we began life. He never liked change. For most of our young adult years he was unsettled by my activities with men, with feminism, and in the world in general. His phone calls sounded like communications from the lower depths I was trying to escape. Perhaps because he knew it would revolt me, he kept me up to date on the latest slurs: Indians were *dots*, blacks were *number two* (shit). "She can sit on my face anytime," was his reaction to seeing a beautiful young woman.

He wanted me to know his world, *the real world* of commerce (he was a realtor) and competition that he entered in order to succeed in the only way the world cared about—by making money. In his world, blacks and women—his family excluded—were objects on which he could vent frustration and have a bit of fun after days of work doing what he may not have truly wanted to do. In this he was only following our father's maxim, a law of life.

"You know the trouble with you, Mimi," he said. "You only do exactly what you want to do."

I told him that wasn't entirely accurate.

"You never left your fucking ivory tower," he told me in another drunken phone call after I'd moved to Montreal. "Up there in Canada with your little chocolate pastries. You don't know anything about how the world really works."

I criticized his attitudes; I tried to change him. Decades later, I stopped trying. I began to hear the suffering beneath his rants. I couldn't help him but I could bear witness and, in so doing, I was able to forgive and, even, love him.

29

Cyberspace

When my friend Samuel friended me on Facebook, I was happily surprised. He's retired to rural Quebec a few hours north of me. We exchange memes, Trump jokes, reacting with thumbs up or claps or hearts to what each other posts. These are fairly standard posts about weather, music, politics, family.

Samuel also included me in his Message Group of mostly relatives and friends, African Americans, some of whom still live near his birthplace north of Rivertown.

What was a casual cyber-social gesture on Samuel's part is, for me, a benediction and a boon. I hover my mouse over tiny faces on features and names I dimly remember from high school. These were the scary black people Connie's mother had warned us against, now comfortably retired, showing photos of their grandchildren.

Members of this cohort repost a wonderful black and white

photo of Samuel's lovely young mother holding his baby brother with Samuel standing nearby in short pants and an argyle sweater. Pre-school. *You must have loved your mother very much. What a beautiful woman.* I write. *Yes I did*, he replies.

Be safe, the African American members of Samuel's cohort wrote last year when he crossed the border to visit his South Jersey relatives. The prayer emoji showed up often.

Last summer, after a family wedding near Rivertown, my husband and I drove up the river road, alongside the new light rail line, in search of a magical childhood place—Cooper's Lane. This was a place Samuel knew too. We'd talked about picking strawberries in the Cooper farm fields, catching minnows in a nearby swamp.

So much has changed, I wasn't sure we could find the turn off for the farm if it still existed. Then an enormous green Turnpike style road sign with blinking lights: COOPER'S LANE. Traffic was all turning right toward the NJ Turnpike. We went left on to a brief patch of blacktop that turned to dirt and then mud. Surrounded by swampland and the calls of birds, frogs and, farther away, chickens, this was the world I'd been seeking.

Cooper's Lane Land Trust read a sign in the swamp.

The Coopers were a venerable Quaker family, pacifists, farmers. They had owned hundreds of acres of fertile riverfront farmland for centuries.

My husband stopped the car at a crumbling Victorian with the sign, *South Jersey Peace Center*.

"Take all the time you want," he said, unfolding the *New York Times*.

I got out and drifted into a dream. Strawberry, blackberry

and blueberry fields. Tractor sheds. Mature hardwoods and swarms of wild roses and grape vines. Several other big houses at a distance and, beyond them, the placid sweep of the river. Crows. A Carolina wren set up its tinkling song. Chickens cooed and browsed around several parked cars. A man passed me on a tractor, lifted a hand in greeting. Far off, a woman in jeans came out of a house and walked to a garden.

I wandered to the edge of a swamp where a set of sagging steps acted as a lookout. I climbed up. There seemed to me no end to the vegetation. A group of young men and women approached, smiled. Yes, they rented the house over there in exchange for farm work.

Oh, did I? That long ago? Yes, it certainly is paradise.

Eventually, as heat began to rise from the open fields, I returned to the car. A deep sadness settled on me. This was the place, the gone paradise before most of this fertile bottomland was reduced to price. This was the beloved old land of childhood. *Get a nigger off the street.*

When I returned to Vermont, I messaged Samuel about Cooper's Lane.

Yeah, he replied. *I spent a lot of time there. Nice people. They let me ride their horses in exchange for cleaning out the stalls.*

Acknowledgements

My gratitude to my beloved and essential friend, Robin Westen, who believed in this project from the start, provided editorial skill and constant inspiration all the way through.
Endless thanks to Hanford Woods , who championed my work for years to friends and colleagues, and whose inspired humor is a life force. Forever, yours.
My affection and thanks to Susan Shein for your meticulous editorial reading of an earlier draft.
I'm grateful to my writing group: Verandah Porche, Richard Wizansky, Todd Mandell, Bart Evans and Lana Golden, who read and discussed an earlier draft of this work.
Thanks to Maria Margaronis who gave an enthusiastic reading of a previous draft.
And my boundless gratitude for the devotion and hard work of my life partner, Rick Zamore
And, finally, to my daughter, Kathryn Jezer-Morton, who is a daily inspiration to me.

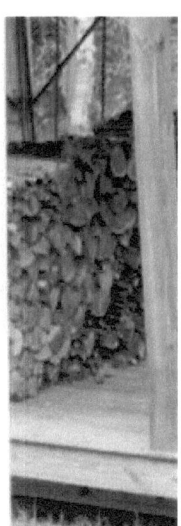

Photo by Ann Elsdon

Mimi Morton is a fiction and a freelance journalism writer. Her fiction has appeared in several small New England literary magazines. She has written freelance for magazines and newspapers in the US and Canada, and on CBC radio. She taught in the English and Humanities departments of Dawson College, Montreal and the English Dept. of Keene State College. She lives in southern Vermont with her husband.

www.ingramcontent.com/pod-product-compliance
Lightning Source LLC
Chambersburg PA
CBHW030335100526
44592CB00010B/706